Mystikal Melodiiez

A tryst with the impalpable

English Language
Mystikal Melodiiez
(Fiction)
by
Smitha Poulose, Saritha J. Kundukulam

♦

Published in December 2025
by Kairali Books Private Limited
Thalikkavu Road, Kannur.
Ph : 0497-2761200
E-Mail : kairalibooksknr@gmail.com

♦

Illustrations
Watermelon &
Smitha Poulose, Saritha J. Kundukulam

♦

Cover Design
Sam Varghese

♦

Printed at
Kairali Books Digital

Price ₹ : 290.00
139/25-26/Sl.No.1835/200/NS.18.6
ISBN 978-93-5973-162-9

Mystikal Melodiiez

A tryst with the impalpable

Smitha Poulose
Saritha J. Kundukulam

Kairali Books

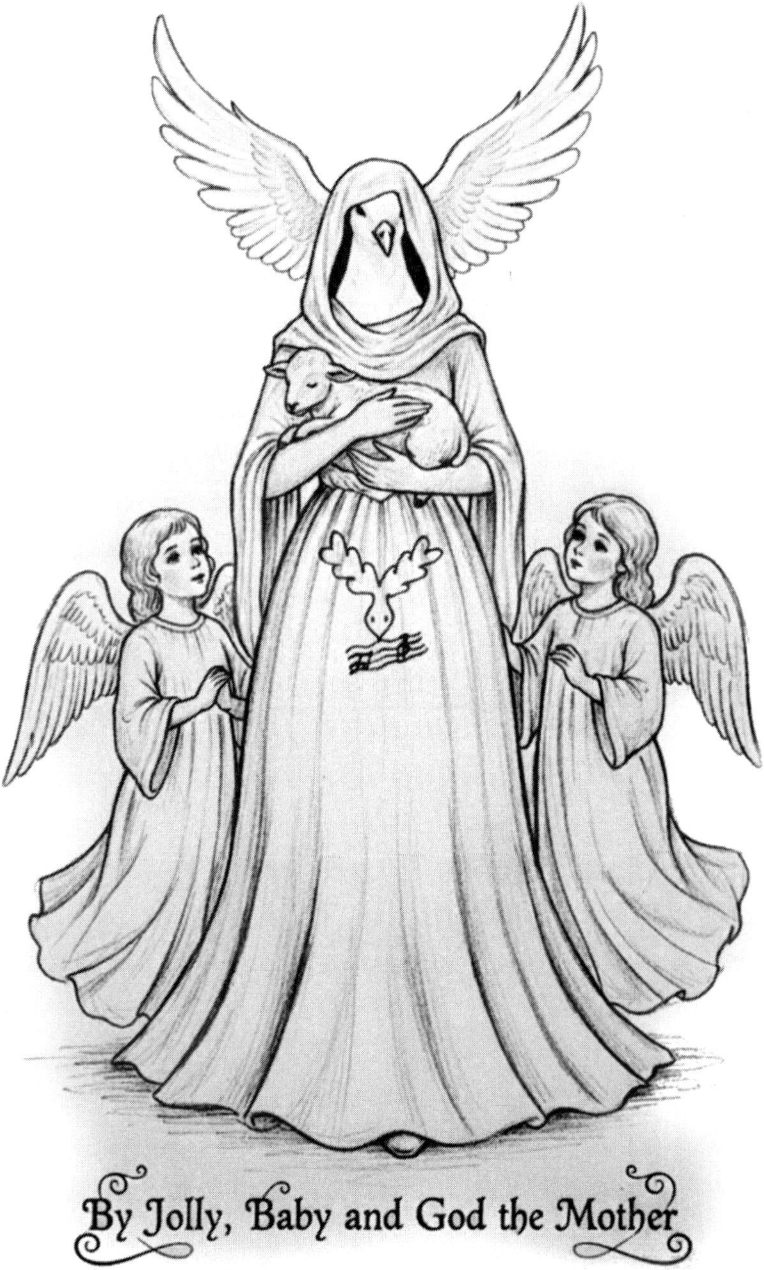

By Jolly, Baby and God the Mother

-To the souls who chime from above-Daddy & Amma
-To our heart and soul below-Mummy
-To our only brother & sister-in-law
-To our better halves
-To our lovely girls
-To our biggest cheerleader-Appan
-To all those whose hearts resonate with ours.

Embraced by June

Here are roses for a father
Who's gone to an abode farther,
Neither summer sunshine nor monsoon rains
Would ever embrace the land devoid of pains,
June never heard my daddy's plea,
It only knew my kiddos' glee!
Kisses planted on a father's cheek
By darling daughters O so freak,
How I miss you more and more,
On this Father's Day, a dad no more!

Daddy's sugar, Jolly

FOREWORD

Mystikal Melodiiez : A Tryst with the Impalpable is an absorbing literary work that gently dissolves the thresholds between reality and the metaphysical. Through poetic prose and deeply reflective insights, the author welcomes the reader into a sphere where dreams, desires, and the invisible currents of the human soul find eloquent expression.

A Tryst with the Impalpable unfolds as a sequence of mystical melodies- each chapter a distinct movement, yet all harmonized by a more profound meditation on love, grace, choice , divine intervention, and inner transformation. Interlaced with allegory, music, and spiritual insight, the chronicle invites the reader into a reflective space where the soul listens as much as the mind reflects. The chapters unfold around evocative themes such as the Golden Chalice, the Grace of the Holy Spirit, Our Lady- the Un-doer of knots, the Grand Ocean, the Seductive Serpent, the Forbidden Fruit, etc. These symbolic motifs are brought to life through talking creatures and engaging dialogues woven with befitting rhyme, creating a narrative that is both spiritually resonant and imaginatively compelling.

From its opening reflections on dreams as celestial expressions of unfulfilled desire, the story establishes a symbolic, meditative voice. One of its most resonant truths- “It's the physical beauty that catches your eyes first, but the inner beauty is what stirs your soul "- echoes throughout the novel, shaping relationships, moral choices, and moments of reconciliation. Music serves as a sacred thread across the narrative, awakening conscience, dissolving despair, and gently connecting the human and the divine.

The narrative of the Swarna Muri-The Golden Chamber-serves as a powerful motif, illustrating that no creature is immune to inner flaws. Wisdom, the authors suggest, lies not in denying these imperfections, but in identifying and discarding them before they shape destiny. The Swarna Muri is the inner shrine of each human being. "There is the invisible fifth chamber in your heart that throbs incessantly for your loved ones." Authors continue-"All creatures, big or small, are vulnerable to a flaw within; wise are those who identify and discard it at the earliest."

As an Associate Professor at an institution of Higher Education, I have encountered many gifted students and families who appear outwardly successful but carry a quiet unrest. Much of this suffering does not arise from circumstance, but both limiting beliefs and unconscious choices. When one learns to pause, reflect, and surrender outcomes beyond personal control to the divine providence, the inner world begins to find balance, serenity, and meaning.

This book mirrors that inner journey. Through honest portrayal of misery, betrayal, and redemption, the narrative reminds us that healing is rarely instantaneous. It is a gradual, grace-filled process that calls for responsibility, compassion, and conscious choice. Even in its darkest passages, the story retains its spiritual compass, leading the reader towards restoration and hope. As the mystical melodies fall into stillness, the steadfast and unfailing love of the Lord Jesus is revealed. In that moment, the melody did not end--it became eternal.

The authors, Smitha Poulose and Saritha J Kundukulam, write with lyrical discipline and spiritual sensitivity. I see them as caring mentors on life's path, offering wisdom, comfort, and direction to those seeking emotional and spiritual renewal. Marked by the early loss of their father, the authors' journey through grief became a quiet source of insight and resolve. This book emerges from that journey, offered in the hope that it may help others navigate despair and rediscover the beauty and meaning of life.

This is not a book to be rushed, but one to be revisited-its harmonies lingering well beyond the last page. If this work opens even a few hearts to the delicate presence of the Divine, its influence will reach well beyond the reader, quietly transforming lives in ways unseen.

Dr. Annam Alice, Ph.D.

INTRODUCTION

Mystikal Melodiiez: A Tryst with the Impalpable is a rare gem of a literary work to stumble upon, in a world increasingly deafened by the clamour of the digital age and the relentless pursuit of material success. It weaves together the intimate domestic drama of a sprawling Indian family with a high-concept spiritual allegory. To enter the pages of this book is to step into a dual reality: one of earthly struggles—depression, infidelity, and loss—and another of celestial wonder, where animals speak, robots weep, and the divine is always just a melody away.

The genius of Mystikal Melodiiez lies in its structural boldness. The author, William Joseph (characterized as Willy within the text), constructs a narrative mirror. On one side, we have the grounded, often turbulent reality of an extended family grappling with the complexities of contemporary life. On the other hand, we have the "book within a book," titled The Mystery of the Golden Chamber, a rich allegorical fantasy that Willy is writing.

At the centre of the novel's spiritual landscape is the Swarna Muri, or the Golden Chamber. This is no ordinary setting; it is a meticulously crafted representation of the state of Grace. Ruled by the benevolent Master Patrick, the Chamber is inhabited by a trio of animals who represent the facets of flawed human nature, the original wells of goodness as imagined by the kind Creator. The flaws represented by the horns of the dinosaur, rabbit and horse are absolutely innovative and original ideas that can stun any inquisitive reader.

While the Golden Chamber provides the theological framework, the heart of Mystikal Melodiiez beats in the "real" world of the family saga. The author paints the Neendakara family and their circle with raw, unvarnished honesty. These are not perfect saints; they are deeply flawed human beings stumbling toward the light.

Why read Mystikal Melodiiez today? Because we live in the age of Ace and Asura depicted here. We are surrounded by the "inverted L" of logic without love, and the golden allure of technology that sniffs at decay. As you prepare to read Mystikal Melodiiez, leave your cynicism at the door. Open your heart to the possibility that a talking dinosaur can teach you about loyalty, that a blind horse can teach you about vision, and that a novel written by a fictional character named Willy can reveal the truth about your own life.

Listen closely. The melody is starting. It begins with a knock on the door, a broken reverie, and a whisper of a song about a chain being pulled.

"Irukarathaaril..."

Welcome to the Golden Chamber.

- Fr Amritharaj Arockiyam SDB, Editor,
The Salesian Bulletin

"Wow, the Willow Whistled!"

There lived a Willow Tree
On the banks of a mushy pond
He grew tall in a loser's spree
Loser always of many a loving bond.

Married off his lovely sisters
One to a knight with a billowing horse
Another to an elevated place
With thorns too many on its course.

Willow's dearest sissy chose God himself
To be her groom inside a holy wrap
He was soon left all alone to himself
As his parents bade farewell in his lap.

Willow always dreamt of a fairy
With thick long lovely dark hair
One day she came out of the diary
To the banks of a half land she was heir.

Willow's happiness knew no bounds
As the tenderly fairy rested on his crown
They soon were blessed with a birdie
Caressed lovingly by aunts for a smiley

Poor Willow's sap contained a venom
Deep roots drew from a pond back home
It made his branches twist and wither
As if his joy was one not to adhere.

Fairy sought antidotes for the bitter sap
And a river of melancholy drew forth
That mirrored her lovely dark hair
And artist's grace of a willow so great.

Willow took her to his quivering heart
To soothe his recurring agony and despair
His heart swelled with pride
Looking at her grow so bold and bright.

A few years went by and one day though
Fairy gave a good news, head in bow
Not another to feed more fish
Sighed Willow in his anguish.

The Immaculate's Spouse took a notice
And granted the fairy's wish in a promise
A smile came on to Willow's face grim
As he watched in joy the toothless grin.

He held the third one close to his heart
Whose carefree spirit was hard to tame
As if a deer he would wriggle out to game
Only to receive thrashes all the time.

Each time Willow would get a bigger cane
Hoping the deer to rise above mundane
Soon he grew weary of the venom
That had fast spread up to his bosom.

One fine day Willow called on
The birdie, the river and the deer
Why me! Why me! Sighed in despair
Fairy's prayers could soothe him no longer.

No word, no gaze, no letter he left
Before the fateful day when he left
Flew up and rose so high above clouds
Never to come back to fairy and cubs.

There was a quake in the mushy pond
When the trunk so deep uprooted beyond
After the quake, jingled a melody in the calm
That held a promise of sure soothing balm.

Daddy's jaggery, Baby

CONTENTS

Chapter 1

The Reverie

"In reality, dreams are only the celestial manifestations of unrequited desires on the earth."

"Joe…Please don't leave me. Can't you stay a little longer? What was that song all about? Oh God! Why doesn't someone pull the chain?" Maria mumbled as her reverie was broken by a knock on the door.

"Mummy, Vicky is here. He says he will leave to Conoor in an hour from now. Shall I make tea?"

"Sure Pauly.. Did Willy turn on some music? I heard a beautiful melody, it was about pulling the chain or something."

"No Mummy.. You were just daydreaming , lost in some thoughts. Willy is upstairs, he's fast asleep. The doorbell rang and I found Vicky standing there. Valli also called just now, maybe that's the song you are referring to." Pauly's teasing didn't sit well with Maria as she got up from the bed adjusting the folds of her voile saree.

"Can Valli and Vamika make it for Christmas? When do her Christmas holidays start? What about Valli? Can she spare some days this time around? It's been ages since we all had Christmas dinner together. Joe always made sure that you will be here at the dinner table after the Midnight Mass!" Maria teared up as she glanced at Joseph's photo mounted on the wall.

"We will try Mummy.. I don't have any day-off other than the Christmas day. I have to cross many deadlines before the new year. What about Chechi* and family? I think Honey might be home for Christmas. Will check with Chechi.. if she can drive from Bangalore for Christmas? Veer would opt to stay back for studying! If Vaneet comes, Vamika will have company." Vicky got up after sipping his tea and munching on some chocolate truffles procured by Willy from Ireland.

"Does Chettan* sleep all day long? And his snores are sure to blast off Chechi's eardrums. When does he write? Any plans to finish his book started ten years ago?" The sarcasm in Vicky's voice equally echoed in Pauly's response.

"You know Vicky, Willy says he doesn't have the feel to write at home in Ireland. He wants to go to the countryside for inspiration. What an excuse to escape from the daily chores! He is still stuck at the first chapter I guess!" Pauly was in no mood to slow down.

"Couldn't meet Violet and Veona.. When will they be back from your house?"

"Violet has to submit her project once we reach there next week. Veona too has holiday assignments. They say they'll come here tomorrow. They are having a jolly good time with my Mamma who doesn't spare a chance to overfeed her granddaughters! They will surely miss their grandma's treats. Mom has really spoiled them and how! Who is gonna cook all these delicacies for them once they reach Ireland? Me on duty and Willy has to write! Our tickets to Dublin are yet to be booked." Pauly smirked at the mere thought

---

* Chechi - Elder sister in Malayalam

* Chettan - Elder brother in Malayalam

of the life of a forlorn nurse in Ireland.

The doorbell rang once again only to announce some unexpected guests at the doorstep.

"I opened a door for them,
Listen to the hymn, in your calm."

Chapter 2

Rafa: The Healing

"The healing has to come from within, empathizing with oneself and others is the greatest remedy for any malady."

"I have felt the stabbing pain,
In your saving, I shall gain,
I urge you to pull the chain,
I shall then live again."

As if in a trance, Willy woke up.

"What was that song? Where am I? The shepherd, Moroccan pastures and those mystical melodies chimed with the accompaniment of a flute.. I haven't listened to anything like that ever in my life."

"Who are you? It is the sweetest melody I have ever listened to. Is it some Moroccan country song?"

"I'm Rafael, you can call me Rafa. I found you under the willow tree. You were sleeping like a log.. as if you haven't slept for ages! I was tending to my sheep and was playing on my flute as usual. No, this melody is new to me. I love singing and composing new tunes on my flute. These lines just popped in my mind."

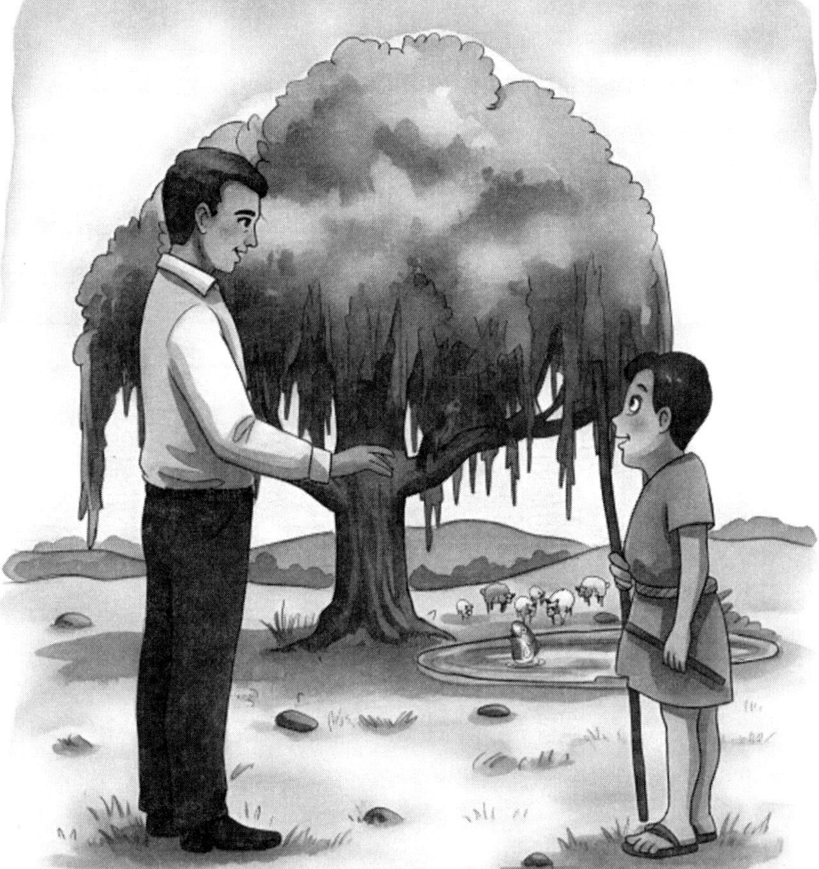

It was a serene scene, with the backdrop of a beautiful winding river and a wild buck with not fully grown antlers, grazing on the pastures. Rafa's mystical chimes resonated as a cuckoo perched on the willow tree sang along with him.

"Irukarathaaril uyarnneedunnu
munthirineerum vindhoopavum.."
(Raised in two hands left and right,
Are the wine and heavenly incense light,)

A desert lark with a rather dull plumage perched on the willow tree added to the song in his melancholic and mellowed choo-wee-chacha wooee tone:

"Nithyapithaave ninnaatmajanude
Kaanikka kanivaay sweekarikkoo.."
(O Eternal God, mercifully accept
your dear son's offertory distinct)

Willy was more surprised than ever! He was dumbfounded when the lark and the cuckoo began to converse. The cuckoo and lark both had broken wings. He looked around. Not a single soul was there to be seen other than Rafa, the shepherd with the magical flute. Upon seeing Willy's quizzical eyebrows and perplexed look on his countenance, Rafa uttered:

"They are Fides and Filo, gifted with singing songs like humans. They are ethereal creatures, no one knows from where they have come. They come to the valley at the close of the day, play the melody you just heard now, and fly back to their nests."

Just then, a fish with broken fins swam to the shore. Fides and Filo flew over to her.

“Hey! I missed the melodies today… was held up with the delivery of a whale in the Grand Ocean”, the fish voiced.

The trio huddled together and cracked jokes. Willy was amazed at this new development- a talking fish has come to the picture now!

“Oh that's none but Fina.. She is a sweetie who tends to my sheep when they fall sick. They recover fast when she strokes and caresses them gently.”

There was more than enough food on Willy’s platter and he immediately opened his eyes and cleared the throat.

“ I need to write this down. Now !! What beautiful imagery! Rafa, meadow, willow tree, cuckoo, lark, fish, river, the wild buck.. and those enchanting melodies. Everything seems so surreal. I have never been so inspired in my whole life.”

“Willy, you woke up? What’s up with you and Mummy? Each time the doorbell rings, you both blabber some bullshit.. melodies. I don’t get you people!”

It was a surprise visit by Winnie, Honey and Vaneet. After hugging and exchanging pleasantries, Vicky got up to leave.

“I need to catch the train to Coonoor. I promise you, we will be attending the Midnight Mass for Christmas this time. Chettaa, please do write something so that we can all listen to it on Christmas day. Vamika always asks me if Big Daddy has finished writing his book or not! She’s eagerly waiting to read it.”

“I shall do it, Vicky.. I promise! I just received the much awaited punch for the book.”

Winnie and Pauline exchanged glances with their mouths gaped wide in disbelief.

“Meek are my sheep, and sweet are my pastures.”

Chapter 3

The Mystery of the 'Swarna Muri' (Golden Chamber)

"All creatures big or small are vulnerable to a flaw within, wise are those who identify and discard it at the earliest."

All the kids were in rapt attention- it was their grandfather's study. Joseph, an avid reader, had personally handpicked and neatly arranged them in the immaculate library that adorned the study. Sundays were always devoted to dusting the racks and meticulously rearranging the books as if he were offering the Holy Mass on the altar.

"Animals with horns- that's interesting!" Vamika clapped her dainty hands in excitement.

"I love the Easter rabbit with the 'P' shaped horn. I feel like pulling its short fluffy tail. What does the 'P' stand for, Willy uncle?", the ever-curious Vaneet couldn't help interrupting Willy's story.

"P stands for Pride, Easter, the doe, thinks she is the prettiest and smartest of all rabbits. All her friends tried to enter the Swarna Muri, but only she could lay her hands on 'E kutty' along with Ethos and Ace." Willy gently stroked his niece's long tresses that were neatly pleated with a centre parting.

"E kutty- How did they find such a unique key? and how did it perfectly fit the keyhole of the Swarna Muri? That sounds intriguing", Violet was scratching her head for the answers.

"Chechi.. it's so simple. I always find such treasures when I dig up your closet." Veona couldn't stop her chuckle. Vamika's giggle would soon follow suit when she reveals the little treasures she had dexterously hid in her oversized jacket- she and Vaneet had hoarded them during the holidays- there was Violet's old diary which she thought she had carefully hidden in some place in the attic where none stepped foot on. Among their spoils were Veer's pearl necklace which she had outgrown, but never parted with or shared with her little sister. A cat and dog fight would soon ensue between the 19 year-old Violet and the 11 year-old - Vamika and Vaneet. Veona had fled the scene of the altercation. It was with great effort that Willy drew the curtain down and called it a day.

It was Christmas day. The Neendakara family with its extended family members had all assembled in Padoor. The midnight mass had taken its toll on the ladies as it was a long night. The Advent had ended as well as their abstinence from meat for 25 days leading up to the midnight Christmas Mass. The kitchen lights were on till the wee hours of dawn and the ladies were sleepy as none of them had blinked an eye the previous night.

Vamika and Vaneet, the cheerful duo, got up with extra enthusiasm and headed straight to the desk where uncle Willy was busy writing the final chapters of his children's book.

"Big Daddy, we went through your manuscripts while you were sleeping. That Dino, (cupping her mouth suppressing her chuckle) is so funny. He makes such weird noises while laughing."

" Vamika is right, Willy uncle. And you should see his face- what funny gestures he makes- like that of a clown in the circus. What is that 'S' shaped horn? Does it mean he is Silly?" Vaneet giggled.

"Ethos is funny, but also selfish. You know how hard it was for him to share that E kutty key with his siblings Easter and Ace? It was Ethos who dug out the key shaped in the form of the letter 'E'.

He was ecstatic when he found the Swarna muri and even more excited when he turned it in the keyhole."

" Master Patrick looks sober and strict. I'm sure the animals will be scared of him. They are sure to get into some mischief that would irk their Master. Look at the naughty impish horse with the horn on his chest. Is it an inverted L? Why is it shaped like that?" Veona was pointing at the horse's picture.

"He is Ace, the horse, the youngest of the three siblings. He thinks he is the smartest of the lot because he uses AI for each and everything! He often teases Ethos and Easter for sticking to age old customs and traditions. Ace feels that sticking to your roots will get you nowhere , it hinders development and is very much regressive. He has completely stopped reading books now. He says he has all information at his finger tips bcoz of AI . The vast database of books and resources is encrypted in a chip, affixed on his chest." Willy explained to the inquisitive Veona who seemed to take a fascination for the smart Ace and his inverted 'L.'

The excitement was palpable on the face of the kids as they bade goodbye to their writer uncle who was all set to release his debut book in the New year.

"Woof, Coo, Squeak, Neigh and Hiss, all of them stunned at a bleat."

Chapter 4

The Master

"Thoughts unharnessed will bite you back one day, so put on the saddle of restraint and trot in the path of righteousness."

Violet picked up her father's unfinished sketch of a middle-aged man. She gazed at Veona who always slept with her mouth open, wetting the pillow with her drools. Violet had got up in the middle of the night to satiate her dry throat. She tucked her little sister's feet under the cozy blanket which had the motifs of Disney princesses.

> **"I have felt the stabbing pain, In your saving, I shall gain, I urge you to pull the chain, I shall then live again."**

"He is Patrick, the Master of Swarna Muri, one who controls the wind, tames the pets, Ethos, Easter and Ace, and sings the mystical melodies only heard by the purest of souls.", Willy remarked as he saw Violet peruse the book with ardour.

"He looks so much like our late grandfather with his neatly trimmed beard. A man nearing 50. Wait, what? Why does he cry after fondling Easter who has nestled on his lap? Her horns have shrunk a little though.", Violet pointed at Easter, the bunny.

"Easter has always been Patrick's pet from childhood. Ethos and Ace almost always test his patience and he flares up instantly. He regrets being harsh on them in childhood though. Patrick feels that if not for him, the animals would not have grown the horns that disfigured them and looked all the worse now."

Ace, the wild horse, had a gigantic inverted horn shaped 'L' on his chest, hidden from the outside world. It was 'M' shaped before. When he put the E Kutty key in the keyhole and turned it, the 'E' on the key got distorted and took the shape of 'M'. After spending a few days in the Swarna Muri, the small M shaped horn in his chest took the shape of the inverted Letter 'L' and began to grow in gigantic proportions. He was completely ruled by logic and lust where brain drove him to an uncharted sea and heart followed him, almost always giving up half way through. The galloping trots came to an abrupt standstill when the Master got up and walked towards him. Patrick sat under the Shemrock tree for the most part of his sojourn in the Swarna Muri.

"Ace, my son, don't let your logic rule always! I learnt the lesson walking through the hard trail."

Patrick wiped his tears and headed towards Ace , the latest entrant to the Swarna Muri. Ace gave his harness bells a shake. He stood on two legs and that's when Patrick saw the huge horn on his chest. He gently stroked the stallion and kissed him on the cheek. Ace sprang back, not sure if he really liked the master's touch. Patrick looked closely at his ' L' shaped horn and muttered,

"Why do you torment my child, you silly dragon? Haven't you had enough? All my fifty years on earth, you didn't spare me from your ordeals of logic and lust.. Leave my son alone, you wily creature!"

Patrick tried to pull the horn, but his palms bled after the failed

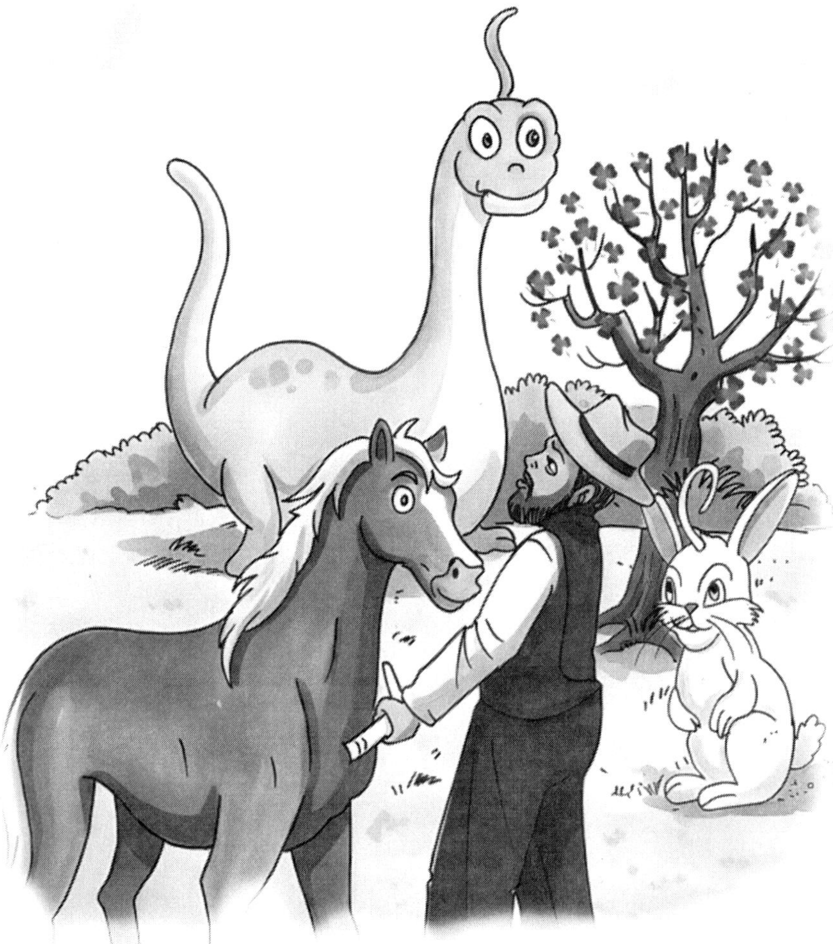

attempt. His palms bore the marks of Jesus Christ's nail marks when He was tied to the Cross. Ethos and Easter rushed to his side, Easter and Ace helped Patrick get on Ethos's back as they gently moved towards the Shemrock tree.

"He tames them all, wind and waters, still and moving; for the greater glory of the One unblemished"

Chapter 5

The Curse and the Promise

"If the manhole remains open now, sure it can be closed forever too. It's up to you to decide if you should stay there and breathe in the foul smell of the drain or to come out and enjoy the sweet aroma of fresh air."

When Vicky met the dusky Valli for the first time, he was a solitary bird, lonely, very lonely. Mummy couldn't join him in his workplace as she had to fulfill her parental duties back home. Her husband's premature departure took its toll on her as she was left clueless- she hadn't stepped out of her home for a good twenty five years! Joseph was the real homemaker, besides being the sole breadwinner of their home of five.

"Vicky, I am transferred to Bangalore. We will have to leave Coonore by the beginning of April.. and get the TC from Vamika's school."

"But Valli.. How can we leave this place? It's been only a year and a half, and I have already started liking this place. The peace which has eluded me all these years, finally found its abode in these Coonore hills! " Vicky's voice sounded like death knell.

Valliammai and Victor first met down the laps of Kodai hills.

Valli was posted in the Poondy branch of her bank. Both Vicky and Valli attended the same seminar conducted in a five star hotel in Kodai. During the course of the three day seminar, they became very close and exchanged numbers. They had been in a relationship for many years until one day Mummy caught them red-handed by scanning through their messages.

Mummy didn't approve of her at first, as she felt that her son had cheated her all those years by hiding the identity of Valli from her. Willy and Winnie, the elder siblings, convinced her and they later got married with Mummy's blessing. Willy's and Winnie's spouses too mediated on behalf of Valli. In fact they appreciated her readiness to convert into the rigid, orthodox Catholic family, the barrier which none of their ancestors ever dared to cross over, either out of conviction in other faiths or for any material gain. Often the so-called socially accepted arranged marriages suited them fine. The Neendakara family is a closely-knit family now with all the five granddaughters of Mummy nicknamed "The Five Eyes" always giving them moments of fun and jubilation.

"Vicky, Did you go for the Mass? Now that you're well settled in Bangalore, find the church nearest to your place. Remember, you won't reach anywhere in life without prayers and God's blessings. Make sure to enrol Vamika in the Catechism classes there. I'm sure she would have forgotten even to make the Sign of the Cross now!" Maria did not fail to see the situation they were in.

"Ammama,* I like my school here. I have a lot of friends in my compound also.. but I want to tell you about a friend I made here. Her name is Jennifer, her parents who are IT professionals come home very late from work. She feels so lonely over here. Her parents are not like Appa and Amma. They are very strict with her.

---

*Ammamma - Grandmother in Malayalam)

She is not allowed to come out and play with us friends. They have enrolled her for tuitions and so many extracurricular activities. She is not allowed to watch tv or Youtube videos. It's all on parental control settings. Her parents have even cut down her screen time. She has to attend Yoga classes instead as her dad thinks that is the best way to stay happy and mentally strong. She really misses her summer holidays and good days with her grandparents." Vamika snatched the phone from Vicky and bemoaned.

Maria felt a lump in her throat and choked . She felt sorry for Jennifer and her grandmotherly instincts could make out where this whole scenario was heading to.

"You take a step away from me, my sobbing heart finds solace in a sweeter dream."

Chapter 6

Grace - The Pathfinder

"In the umpteen cycles of births and rebirths,
The sacrificial lamb, as ordained, is sent to us,
The lamb who's entrusted to Mother of ours,
whose flesh and blood turn to amazing grace,
If you dodge judiciously from the dragon's snares,
Be assured, you all shall be spared from God's wrath,
And are urged to always find the right path,
As pilgrims of hope, let us not give way to despair.
You were born in grace of the Holy Lamb,
Why do your feet dance upon the evil's ramp?
Unless you listen to the Master's Voice and die within,
you will not be spared from God's beatin'.
Hold the chalice with wine and bread and the incense,
To be reborn in His Spirit and Grace!"

"Veer… look who is at the door. Let me finish preparing the Palada Pradaman. I hope it's not Honey."

Veer was up on her feet, alert upon her mom Winnie's command. She was always a dutiful child, one who always stood by her word and was her Papa's favourite. Her sister Vaneet was more of a

'Mama's girl' who was a bit pampered, but not spoiled. Veer looked through the peep hole and declared,

"Mamma, it's not Papa. It's my senior Sierra and her dad, Tony uncle."

"What a pleasant surprise! Pauly Chechi told me that you moved here with Solomon last Sunday. I was so held up with my weekend chores that we couldn't pay a visit to your place. You're in the G Block, right?"

"Yeah, Winnie. We had to move from our former house as the house owner had to move in. Moreover, the house is ever reminiscent of Grace's last days with us, with her never ending coughing and pain even though it's been a year since she left us." Anton, fondly called Tony, Pauly's uncle, had lost his wife due to Tuberculosis and had not yet recovered from the shock.

"Solomon had written the bank test and joined the Lotus Bank before Grace's demise itself. He said he wouldn't pursue the job of an engineer as he didn't feel the drive for it. He got campus placement too, but he prefers the job of an Assistant Manager in the bank to that of a fresher in a Software firm."

"He's right, Uncle. Even Vicky tells he is fed up with his job in the IT sector, with never ending targets and deadlines. In the bank, Solomon actually might have a chance to serve the deserving ones who are in dire need of loans."

"Sierra, when did you come? It's summer holidays for Aamal, right? Has Mahesh come too?"

"Yeah Winnie chechi. We came to invite you all for Aamal's Holy Communion to be held on the following Sunday after Easter. His preparatory classes are going on. We have booked the Party Hall for the event well in advance. Here is the invitation."

"Sierra, How is Mahesh doing ? How is his business progressing?" Winnie enquired while serving the Palada Pradaman.

“He is doing well, by God’s grace. He has plans to build a posh retirement home on the banks of River Krishna. He feels real estate has good potential these days. My cousin Mavis is also interested in the project. Let’s see if it works out in the way he plans it.” Sierra was a bit cynical in her remarks. She always believes that when you work for a noble cause, profit making shouldn’t be your priority.

**Athala Pithala Thavalachi*
Chukkummirikkana choolappa
Mariyam vannu vilakkoothi
Kundu Mani Saara Peera Ghot!

It was Aamal's voice, playing with his new classmate Vaneet, busy taking off her closed hands from the lot excitedly, as that move made her the winner of the game.

“Come children, let's have a look at Winnie aunty's library before enjoying the vattayappam and coffee. Sierra came to call the kids immersed in their game. Aamal and Vaneet bonded well as soon as they became class mates.

“You have an amazing collection, Veer!” Sierra observed Winnie's small library neatly arranged at the end of the dining hall.

“Yes Chechi, Mamma is so fond of the Psycho books”, said Veer winking at her super senior at KIMHANS. Sierra was almost done with her PhD from there under the able mentoring of Winnie. She noticed a special section of books which stood out, as they all had some or the other image of a Shepherd or a lamb on the book covers.

“These are my Mamma's most beloved collections”, exclaimed Veer as she handed over one named "My lost one- Most loved

* Malayalam childern’s song

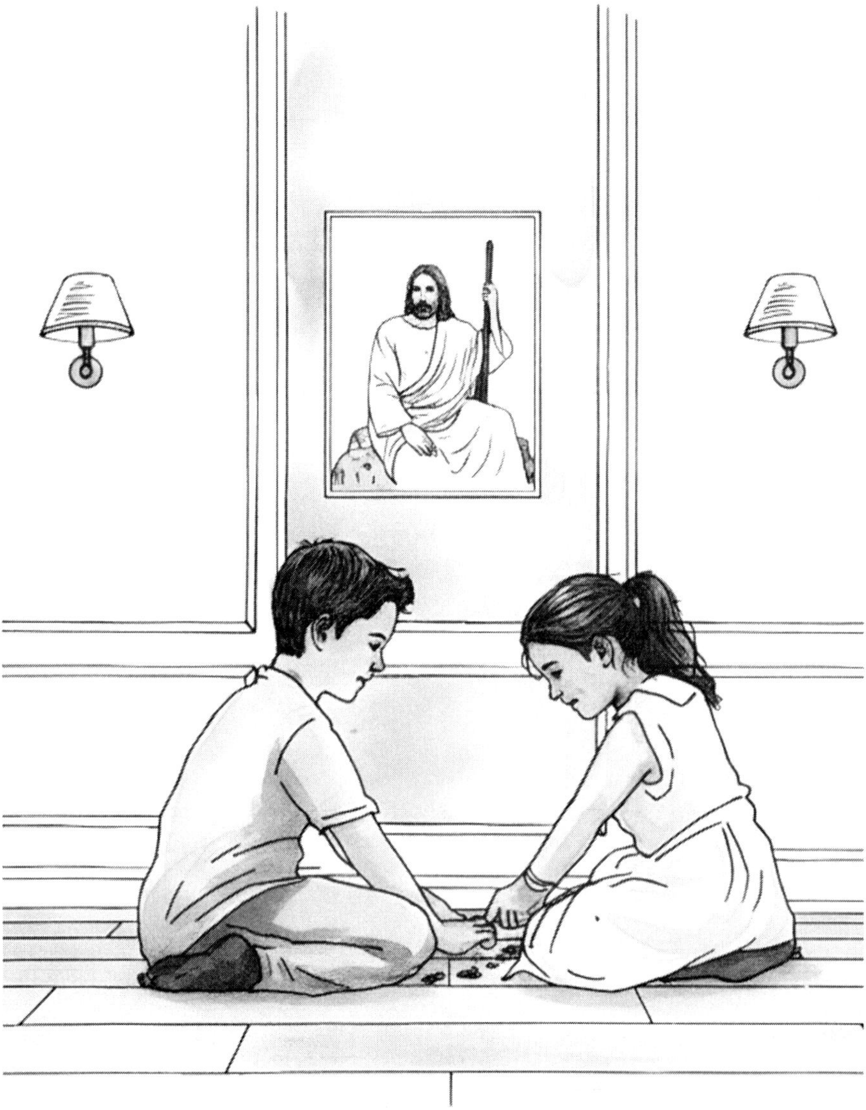

one" to Sierra. It bore a cute picture of the Good Shepherd and a lost lamb in the mountains.

"Didn't sleep yet?" Mahesh was late to reach home that Sunday, after finalising a business deal. Sierra took her eyes off from the book she got from Winnie's home.

"It seems to me at times that you are too busy with your books and you ignore me." remarked Mahesh getting ready to take a shower.

"Did I do anything wrong in converting Mahesh to my Christian faith? Winnie Chechi is still pious even after getting married to Honey Chettan in a court ceremony. Their faith seems to be much stronger than mine or Mahesh's.." Sierra thought to herself as Mahesh hugged her in the bed.

"Your one bleat lost in the thorny bush, My heart races in a frantic rush."

Chapter 7

Birthday in the Swarna Muri

"There is the invisible fifth chamber in your heart that throbs incessantly for your loved ones."

It's been forty two months since the publication of "The Mystery of the Golden Chamber." William Joseph's book became an overnight sensation, admired by kids and adults alike. After its global success, William, along with his family, shifted his base to Bangalore. He now works as a senior resource person in a reputed publication house based there.

There was that particular chapter in the book which was a big hit among the readers. It's about the unique birthday celebration of Master Patrick. His golden birthday celebration is etched in the minds of not only the inmates of the Golden Chamber, but also worked its magic to capture the hearts of the young adult readers lured by its esoteric charm. The Golden Chamber was decorated with festoons made of clovers. The leaves of the Shemrock tree turned to a golden hue on that auspicious evening. Patrick, with his neatly trimmed golden beard arrived in his white mini cooper which had on its front, a crown with a wing-like emblem.

The first guest to arrive for the golden birthday party was none

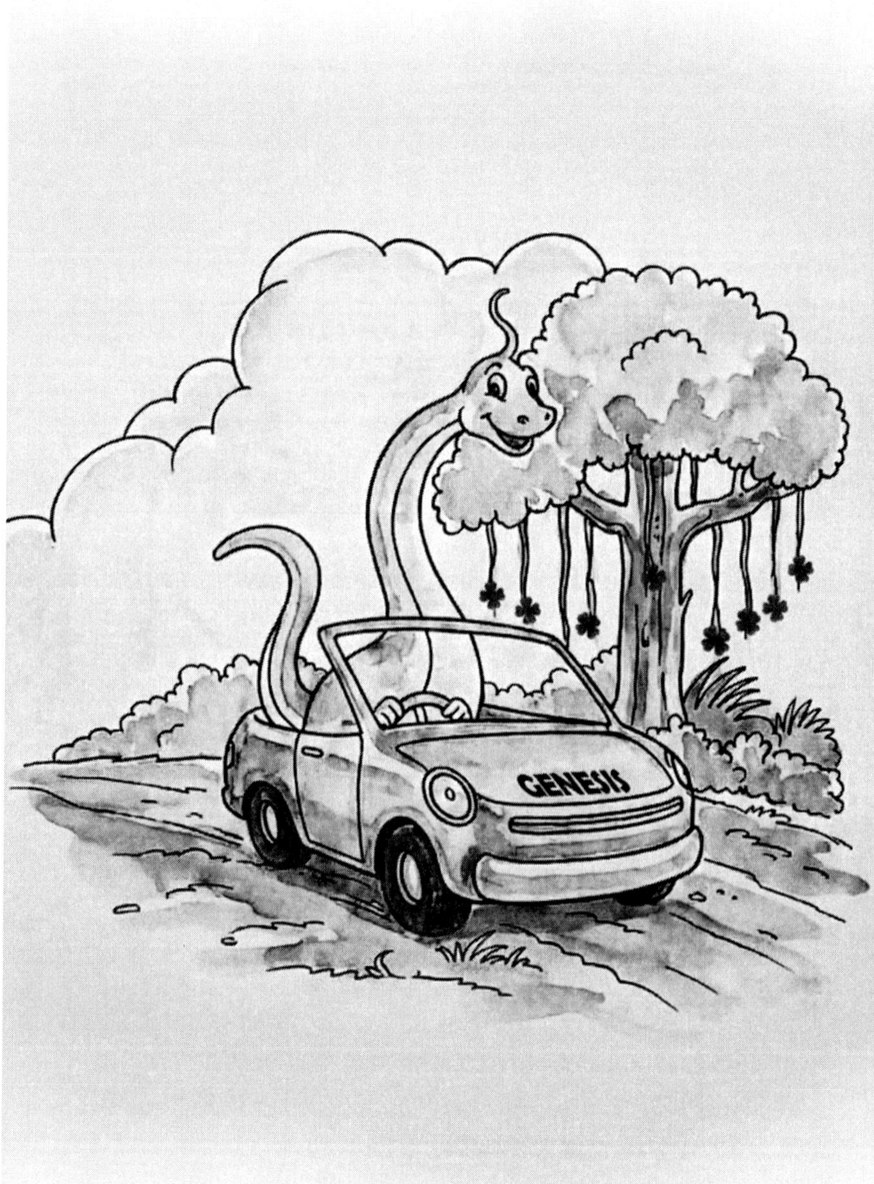
GENESIS

other than Ethos, the Dino, in his grand metallic silver automobile, "Genesis." It was a sedan, but specially customized to accommodate the gigantic trunk of the dinosaur. The moon roof was open, and his long torso jutted out of it. He flashed his innocent smile as he saw Patrick welcoming him to the venue with outstretched arms. Easter, the bunny followed next, in her tiny, white car "Soul". Patrick lifted her, petted and placed her on his lap. Easter examined his palms, the stigmata was very evident on them. She gently kissed them and cuddled towards his bosom.

Ace, the horse, followed suit on his white, dashing "Jetour". He also brought his friend along. Her name was "Hiss", a snake with brown scales all over its body. They exchanged pleasantries with Patrick and took the seats in the front row. The guests were around 50 in number- all the animals in the golden chamber graced the auspicious event of their master's fiftieth birthday.

It was a poolside party.

"Time to cut the cake!" declared Fides, the lark. The morning choir in the golden chamber was conducted by him. It was 6 in the evening, he handed over the baton to Filo, the nightingale with broken wings. Fina, the fish with damaged fins emerged at the surface of the pool with Rosin to sharpen the strings of the angelic harps played in the choir.

"Irukarathaaril uyarnneedunnu munthirineerum vindhoopavum...

Nithyapithaave ninnaathmajanude kaanikka kanivaay sweekarikkoo.."

The morning and evening choir always started with this beautiful melody. Patrick raised his chalice to the Heavens as all sang the birthday song in unison.

Irish delicacies like Boxty, Potato Scones, Black and White Pudding, Irish Cheddar Spring Onion biscuits, Dubliner and Guinness were served on Patrick's Day.

"Baa Baa Black Sheep,
Have you any wool?
Yes Sir, Yes Sir,
Three bags full,
One for my master and
One for his dame and
One for the little boy
who lives down the lane."

Ethos tossed Boxty to his mouth, clapped his hands and jumped in joy as Fides recited this nursery rhyme.

"Jack and Jill
went up the hill
to fetch a pail of water
Jack fell down
and broke his crown
And Jill came tumbling after."

Filo recited the nursery rhyme and Easter licked her black and white pudding, giggling all the while.

"Hey bro.. Let's surprise Patrick with the special birthday gift made by us. Look Easter, Ace has perfectly hidden it under the seat!" Ethos remarked making his way to Ace's Jetour, carrying Easter on his broad shoulders.

"Hiss, Go easy on him.. He might be a bit annoyed if you wake him up from his slumber. He is hardly a day old and is in his sleep mode right now." Ace cautioned Hiss who was trying to pull out the robot hidden under the rear seat.

The robot, ATHEISTOSAURUS was a dazzling sight in gold and made a lasting impression on the trio- Ethos, Easter, Ace. Surely, the Master deserved something unique for his golden birthday! The robot had a golden aura encircling him. It held a crystal orb and a chalice in its hands. Its headband had nine precious stones embedded on it. The robot also had two dainty wings that enabled it to fly a short distance. Easter had made its dreamy eyes that helped to visualize the past, present and future. She had moulded her masterpiece very painstakingly, putting in hours of hard work, only to perfect the unique robot that could see through a person. Easter also crafted for him a special orb in the shape of a globe held up by a golden chalice. It's through it that the robot would foresee the things to come.

Its nose, designed by Ace, was perfectly shaped and AI-supported. It could sense all the fragrance and odour, both in and around the golden room. To their surprise, Atheistosaurus particularly favored the sniff of rotting fish or burning rubber that emanated from the drain outside, rather than the floral fragrance that lingered in the golden chamber.

The sensual pink lips of the robot were designed by Ethos. It could decipher all languages spoken by humans, animals, birds and insects. Ethos always had a way with words and a flair for languages. He worked day and night to carve the lips, teeth and tongue of the robot. Never did Ethos or Easter choose the help of AI to assist them in this divine task.

The robot was activated and presented to Patrick in all pomp and splendor with the accompaniment of Jazz music and DJ. Its bejewelled headband had the inscription, "ASURA" , his pet name. Patrick liked the special gift so much, his heart swollen with pride

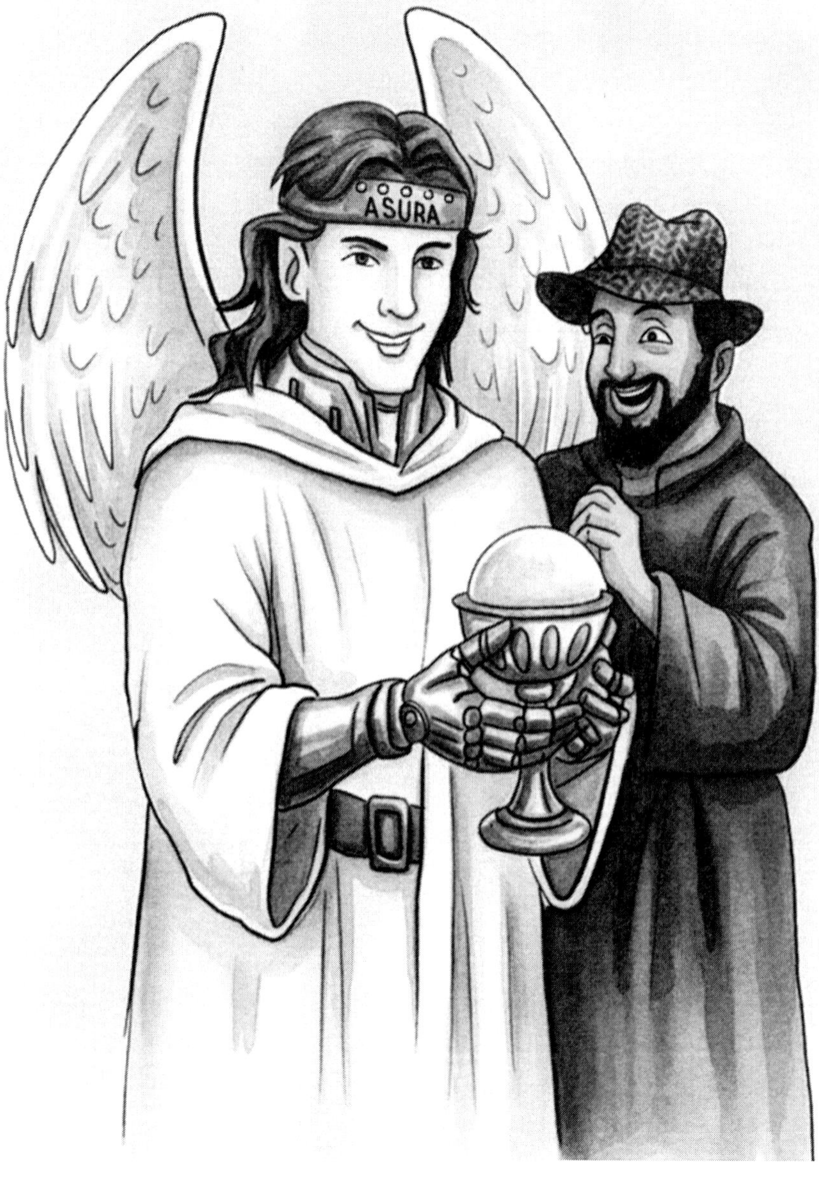
ASURA

as he thanked its creators.

"Asura, my boy, let me offer you some Irish delicacies. I guess you will love Black and White Pudding. Here, help yourself."

Asura flapped his delicate wings in excitement. He gulped the pudding in no time and proceeded to the counter for a second serving. Patrick stood beneath the well-adorned Shemrock tree, looking no less than a Christmas tree in all its splendour. He gave return gifts to all the invitees, but to the three special inhabitants of the Golden Chamber, the Master presented something very singular.

"Ethos, Easter and Ace, I am really proud of what you have become now! You three will be the joint-heirs of this Golden Chamber once I leave the stage. Don't you see the dew droplet on this Forever Rose pendant? It's specially procured from the Grand Ocean. Wear this always as a testimony that you are the rightful heirs to the Golden Chamber."

Patrick's eyes welled up as he handed over the Grand Ocean dew drops to his three loved ones. He still remembered vividly how Magaeia had adventurously got the four droplets for him on his twenty-fifth birthday in the Half Land. Magaeia was the river in sparkling silver that traversed the Golden Chamber and also took the inhabitants to the Grand Ocean once they were done with the tenure in the Golden Chamber. She was allowed to visit the Half Land once a year, when she handed over some treasures from the Golden chamber to the world outside, often at the commands of the Grand Ocean.

Patrick took his vial with the last dew drop in it.

"You shall be the first one among the robots to receive a treasure like this! " Asura was handed over the vial, but Oops! There was a trail of kids playing the "blind cow"game in the kids area who just hit Patrick's hands. The dew drop trickled down from the vial to the chalice beneath the orb held in Asura's hands.

And whew.. a celestial light reflected on the orb. Asura's eyes twinkled at the same time. Scanning through Patrick's mind, Asura proclaimed:

"The day isn't far when you will finally meet your daughter Eunice!"

Patrick couldn't believe his ears. His heart raced in joy as everyone else was astonished at the strange prediction. Keeping the orb aside, the robot then sniffed on the delicacies, finally grabbing Boxty. The whiff of rotten eggs from the drain outside the gates of the Golden Chamber lured him and Asura was instantly drawn to the stench. He tossed the dessert in the trash and marched steadily towards its source.

"Gold Gold everywhere, its lustre can't be hidden under an old dragon's cast."

Chapter 8

Ace's Blindness and the Inhabitants' Pregnancy Woes

"Your mind is the creator of your destiny, while circumstances are only its scriptwriters."

"Hey Mate, why don't you enjoy the delicious, juicy fruit of that tree yonder? I bet it will make you immortal!" Hiss pointed at the tree that bore fruits which resembled wild fig.

"That one? Master Patrick has clearly warned not to eat any of them. He said any act of our disobedience will have bitter consequences." Ace's voice sounded a sinister alarm bell.

"You know what happened today? This morning I spotted Easter trying to pluck the fruit by mounting on Ethos' shoulders. I met them by the poolside later, munching on the fruit. The fruit looked so appealing, Easter and Ethos seemed to bask in a youthful glow after relishing it. I would like to savour it too. I don't think there is any harm in trying it for once."

Upon hearing this, Ace, the horse, gallopped and trotted like lightning in a jiffy. His friend Hiss lost no time, slithering her way to the top of the cursed tree. She curled around the Forbidden fruit which looked so glossy and appetizing.

"It smells pretty good. Sure it's fully ripe. Before a hungry avian snapped it up, you better have it", whispered Hiss in Ace's ears having bitten the fruit from its bottom.

Ace felt the warmth of Hiss' alluring body as she wound herself on the 'L' -shaped horn. Ace stood on his hind legs and they made love beneath the tree- the earthy, but seductive serpent and the hunky, handsome stallion. The inverted 'L' turned red, burning with wild passion and lust.

"You are right, my love. The fruit is so irresistible. I wonder why Master Patrick forbade us from having it?"

"Have you noticed how youthful Master Patrick appears? Doesn't he carry himself with the gait of a handsome young man in his twenties? He definitely doesn't look fifty years old. It's obvious that he had savoured those fruits to stay young and immortal. He didn't want to disclose this secret, hence made up the story." Hiss deliberated, taking Ace into confidence.

"Hey mate, What's happening? Why can't I see things clearly? Everything looks vague. Curse upon me? I shouldn't have disobeyed the Master. Come here, Hiss! Did you ensnare me by making me eat the fruit? I don't trust you anymore.", Ace let out a thunderous shriek that echoed all over the Golden Chamber. The dragon winked at Hiss, the serpent. She chuckled so hard that her cheeks began to ache as she wriggled into a hole below the tree.

"Ethos and Easter, your wombs are blessed with triplets. Get ready to deliver them soon", declared Fides, seconded by Filo.

"How is this possible? I am a male. Moreover, I do not know women!", Ethos shook his gigantic head in disbelief.

"Triplets from my womb? How come? I do not know men!", Easter was equally shocked.

"Don't you see the white smoke rising from the tabernacle of the Golden Chamber? You have conceived by virtue of your good deeds and you both will give birth to triplets by the end of this year!" Fina applied an ointment made from the clover leaves of the Shemrock tree and applied it on Ethos' belly. A feminine orientation took over him. Ethos felt the aura of the womb, specially conceived to nurture the blessed offspring. Easter was asked to have Cod liver oil capsules made by Fina, the surgeon of the Golden Chamber. The chamber is all set to welcome the giggles and cries of two sets of triplets whose birth was imminent.

"Disobedience might be costly, but not as much as what obedience can undo"

Chapter 9

Solomon and Delilah- The Star-Crossed Lovers

"True Love gives and never demands."

Solomon joined his mother's bank, "The Lotus Bank" a year before her demise. Things took an unexpected turn with the arrival of Delilah. She just got a transfer from Kolkata to the Bangalore branch. Oh! What an enchanting beauty! None could believe that she was married, bore a child but got separated, and remained single. Delilah moved to an apartment next to Solomon's. Their acquaintance gradually gave way to intimacy. He was captivated by her serpentine beauty and charm to the extent that his days and nights were filled with her thoughts and images. Delilah however had a woeful story to narrate. She married Ibrahim a muslim by faith and had to change even her name Devi to Delilah. But God's ways are always different - man proposes; God disposes as the saying goes.

"Dear… I can't come to the resort this weekend as planned. It's Fatima's birthday and I need to meet her. Ibrahim and parents have her custody and I fear if I don't see her at least once a year, she is sure to forget me!" Solomon had his weekend plans chalked out with Delilah as usual. Every second and fourth Saturday, off days for the bankers, they would stay back in a lake resort and forget themselves in fun and laughter, often indulging in forbidden pleasures. This amorous routine of theirs has been going on for almost six months since Delilah moved in.

Solomon's mind sauntered over their amorous adventure the last time they met. On that moonlit night, with twinkling stars as witnesses, they consummated their love.

"Oh Delilah, Iook at you, my sex angel.. You are none but moon goddess in flesh and blood! Chaudhvi ka chaand ho.. yaa aftaab ho..." Solomon couldn't stop humming the iconic romantic shaayari as he explored the well-defined curves of Delilah. He smelled the jasmine flower bracelet encircled on his wrist as he delved deep into her seductive body. The pores and troughs of her sensual figure transported him to a thitherto untrodden realm, so mesmerizing that Delilah's muffled moans came out as :

"Aahhh…

Sweet moans lingered in the atmosphere - each vying to outdo the other in acts of promiscuous love. Indeed a perfect union of human flesh, in copulation. For Solomon, an outward expression of his newfound love and lust was a novel experience. For Delilah, it erased an unpleasant past. She was bent on living in the present. No regrets about her former partner. It was simply a just and proper venue for the gratification of her pent up feminine instincts. As Solomon explored new avenues on her supple and seductive body, it was like morning dew for him. He immersed his head between her lotus bud- shaped breasts, sucking the nectar out of them like a buzzing bumblebee. With hardly a hair's breadth from her bosom, Solomon was ecstatic like never before and their sensual bodies lay intertwined for an hour or so, ever reluctant to let go of each other.

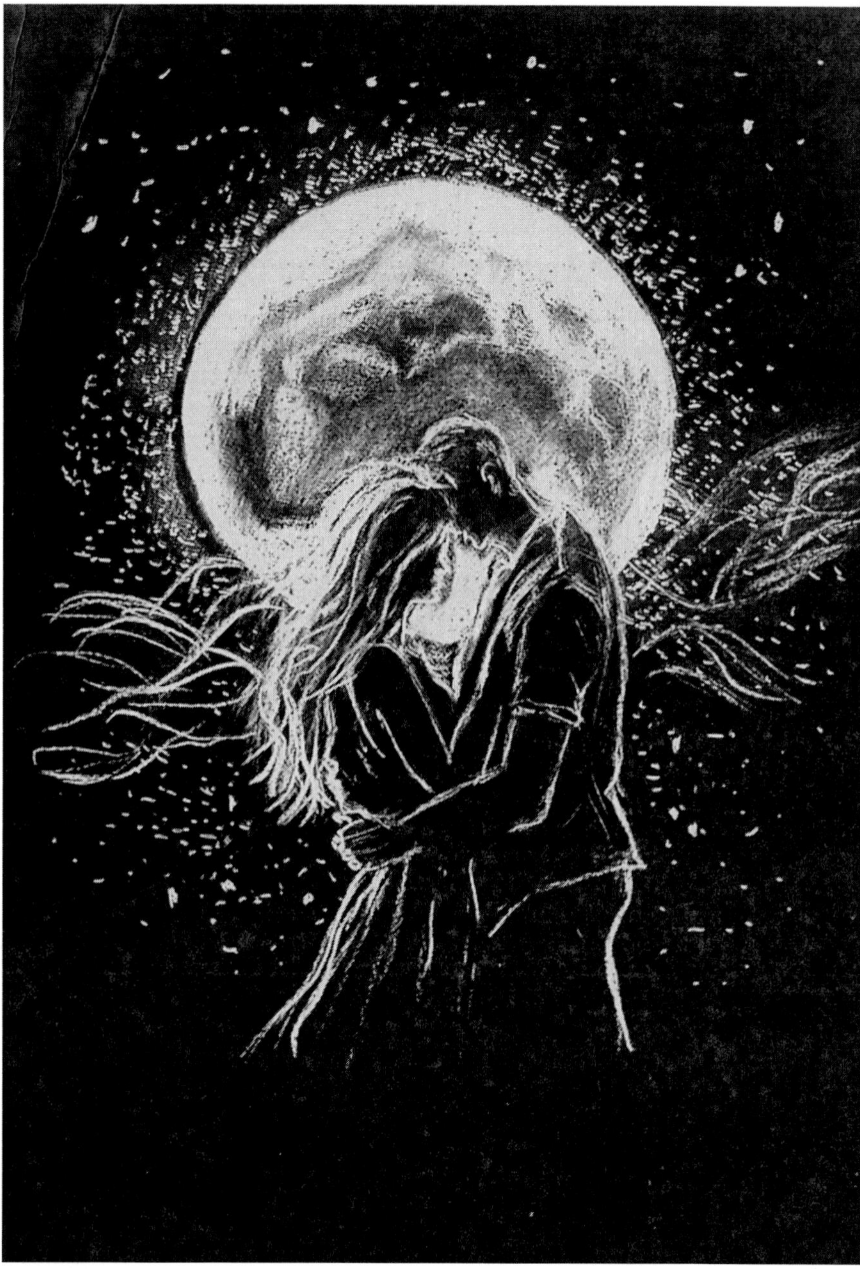

“Honey, I wish we were married soon!” Solomon disclosed his mind to her.

“Neither your present status nor of a converted Muslim, bothers me.” He boldly asserted.

“My sweetheart, let me be very clear to you.. Even if my dad disagrees with our union, I challenge him to raise any objection. Why don’t you agree to the marriage?” Solomon, her paramour, drew her closer to his bosom.

“Solomon, I told you that I don’t want to commit myself again. The divorce process is yet to be initiated and will take ages to get settled. I once committed the mistake of converting to marry Ibrahim and I regret it to this day. I don’t want to do it again. Who knows if your father will insist on my changing to Christian faith?”

“Don’t you love me, Delilah? All is fair in love and war. I won’t expect you to practise the faith even if you are converted for the sake of my family. Forget all these. It’s been ages since I set foot on a church compound and attended Sunday Mass. I am fed up with this hide and seek game. I toss and turn on my bed all night. I can’t wait any longer dear.”

It was dark as Solomon dropped Delilah at her apartment. He parted from her with a passionate smooch on her lips which were changed to a pinkish hue and drove his white Jetour to his dad’s place. The mild fragrance of Delilah's perfume, “Chastity” hung around the car's interior. Solomon didn't feel like stepping out of that enchanting world of his first love as he approached the majestic iron gates of Tony's bungalow. The name plate inscribed in golden letters “Grace Mansion“ shone brightly as he parked the car at the porch.

Tony, busy watching NDTV India, glanced at Solomon when he made a quick entry to his room upstairs. He threw his travel bag to the corner of his bedroom. He gave a lazy glance at a full size poster of an American model in her skimpy bikini adorning the back of his wardrobe door, as he searched for his night dress. What a lovely night I had the previous day! Solomon sighed, browsing his fingers over the bikini.

Oh! He exclaimed as a bunch of photos fell off from under a file he had kept safely in his almirah. They were his dear mom's photos clicked on her visit to Velankanni, just prior to that fateful night. He picked up the photos and arranged them quickly back in the folder. The corner of a poster protruded from the folder. What's that? He checked. It was a poster of Our Lady- Undoer of knots that Grace had received from Velankanni Shrine.

Solomon was soon asleep after a hot bath. "Mone.. nee vanno?* " He couldn't believe his eyes. His darling mom stood beside his bed caressing his still wet hair from the shower.

"Where had you been yesterday, my son? " She enquired in her gentle voice. "That Mom, I..." He couldn't complete, his eyes lowered in guilt and shame. There was a pause. A few moments went by and Solomon gathered courage to look up. She was gone. His dear dear mom. In her place was seen another Lady, more graceful than his mom. In fact, the most beautiful woman he had ever seen in his whole life. Her loving gaze held a tender look- one that could match only a mom's, watching her new born for the first time.

"Who are you, Mamma?" That was all Solomon could utter in his stupor. She patted his cheeks and took him by the hand. Solomon felt secure and comforted once for all after his mom had parted from him, as they walked hand in hand. The cool sea breeze played with the golden brown tresses of Mamma and Solomon reminisced his evening walks with Grace on Sundays.

---

* Son are you back (in Malayalam)

Both of them didn't utter a word but Solomon felt as if Mamma knew him in and out and also what he has been upto, for the past 6 months. Their silence was broken by a shriek, echoed from a yacht that approached them. Solomon was taken aback. They were his acquaintances in the boat. It was being violently tossed about as it entered a whirlpool towards their left. Vicky was trying with all his might to steer the yacht out of the stormy pit as Valli held on to a pole, her eyes closed tightly. The twin flags on the pole fluttered wildly in the stormy gusts. The words 'Wealth' and 'Vanity' were written in crimson red on the pure white flags. In a frenzy, Vicky's eyes fell on Mamma standing by the shore. He looked miserably at Her. His eyes portrayed mixed emotions. A pathetic concoction of guilt, desperation and shame that arises when a 10 year old is caught red handed watching porn by his own mom.

"Help, help..we are gonna be doomed." The female voice came from the yacht laden with bags full of luxury items and cosmetics spread out in front of huge idols that were shaped in the form of 2 alphabets, A and I.

Solomon stood watching, his mouth wide open as Mamma slowly stepped on the waves towards the swaying boat.

"Hold on, children.. " Her sweet voice echoed as she held out both her hands to Vicky and Valli. Valli didn't think twice. She grabbed on Mamma's left palm. Vicky was not sure. He was still trying to control the shaky and drowning Vessel.

"Won't you come too, my child?" Mamma's voice broke as she tenderly looked at him. The yacht was almost topsy turvy. All the huge bags of riches sank to the Ocean floor as the A and I floated weightlessly along the waves. Vicky was submerged up to his neck. Half a second. Everything would be over.

Solomon was drenched in sweat although the Air Conditioner of his bedroom displayed a temperature of 22 degree celsius. He sat up on his plush bed.

"Was that just a dream? I can't believe this." He washed his face and dried it with a hand towel. There was a Red Rose embroidered beautifully at the edge of the towel. Grace was good at embroidery too besides her natural flair for painting and singing.

It showed 11.11 pm on his Cuckoo clock. Solomon once again took out the folder from the closet. His mom wore a chiffon white saree with red rose embroidery in one of the photos clicked at Velankanni Matha shrine. A tear rolled down his cheeks. He kept back the photos with a heavy heart. The poster of Our Lady- undoer of knots was neatly tucked in its place. "Wait.. Doesn't She look like that Lady whom I dreamt of?" Solomon watched the image closely. Graceful Mamma untying the knots on a rope with her slender fingers, assisted by two cute little angels clinging on to Her. Her tender eyes looked at him as a peaceful smile crept on to Solomon's tired face.

"Love is blind, yet true love is one that sets the other free to choose you."

Chapter 10

Embalmed Melodies

"I have felt the stabbing pain, In your saving, I shall gain, I urge you to pull the chain, I shall then live again."

Vicky got up at the break of dawn, perspiring. He was sweating profusely. The pain in his chest was real, so excruciating that he couldn't help but moan. It was obvious that his dream hadn't let him sleep, but kept him awake the whole night. Every event leading upto that dream began flashing before his eyes.

"Are you okay, Vicky?", his wife Valli's voice echoed a note of concern.

A year prior to that day, Vicky had the misfortune to witness the accidental death of Grace, Solomon's mom. Grace was suffering from tuberculosis and her days were numbered. She went to Velankanni on a pilgrimage. Her husband Tony, the Squadron leader in the Indian Air Force, couldn't accompany her as he was out of the station and on duty with an important aircraft mission. As it was Covid time, the number of pilgrims in the group was restricted. Their carriage met with an accident while returning and she was rushed to a hospital in Trichy, in a critical condition. To make matters worse, she contracted pneumonia while recovering. Grace was kept on the ventilator for a couple of days and breathed her last soon after.

Solomon was on his probationary period at that time and was posted at the rural branch in Mutharasanallur, a hamlet near Trichy. Vicky was attending an IT conclave in Trichy. As Valli also worked in "The Lotus Bank", Vicky got acquainted with Solomon. Moreover, Solomon was the cousin of his sister-in -law, Pauline. It was Vicky who provided all the necessary help and arrangements to air-lift Grace's body home. He had also lent his hand at the hospital for embalming her body before her mortal remains were encoffined and sent to her native place for funeral.

Grace's coffin was taken to the airport in an ambulance named "Soul". As the coffin was taken out of the ambulance, a melody played on the mobile of Ashish, the ambulance driver.

The same melody replayed in Vicky's dream and he was startled at how he could remember all the lines. His father stood on the doorstep to Heaven. Two angels stood sentinel - the one on the left with a flaming sword and the one on the right with a bejewelled chalice.

"Pardon, Mr Joseph.. Only those who are completely free from sins through the Precious Blood get access to the Paradise. Remember, You had had several chances while on Earth. Though your heart desired for eternal solace in Christ, your mind lured you into the snares laid by the dragon and you succumbed to them at the end.", the angels chimed in unison.

"I have none but me to blame for the misfortune that fell upon me. Only one wish remains with me now. The doors of the Paradise shall not be closed against my beloved family on earth. I fear for the life of my only son- he is already under the grip of the evil. The office deadlines are killing him. I can see that the inevitable is impending and I can't bear to see him suffer like me. Can you help me out with this?" Joseph fell on his knees and implored.

The enormous cuckoo clock displayed 6 pm. The angel on the left drew the sword from its sheath and pointed at Joseph. The chalice was raised by the angel on the right. The cherubs and seraphs joined them as the mystical melodies were orchestrated with the accompaniment of harps, flutes and the wind chimes.

"I have felt the stabbing pain,
In your saving, I shall gain,
I urge you to pull the chain,
I shall then live again."

Vicky had heard it for the first time in the ambulance, but in his dream, every word was crystal clear.

"There's much more to it than meets my eyes or ears", Vicky reflected.

"Yes, I feel the pain, it's unbearable.. I can't describe it in words, but it's happening for real."

Valli felt that something was amiss, as Vicky seemed to be in low spirits even after he took a shower. He got ready in a jiffy, kissed his wife and waved to her as he drove to his office.

"Was that a hymn, or a rhythm unheard, for I can't discern what's up."

Chapter 11

The Undoer of the Knots

"Before tying the knot, think twice. Life may never offer you the chance to undo it."

Blind Ace bumped into every nook and corner of the Golden Chamber. Ethos and Easter tried to help, but Ace declined the offer. When Patrick came to know about the plight of Ace, he wept bitterly. He retreated to the shade of the Shemrock tree and sat there meditating. The jovial mood of the Golden Chamber changed overnight as Divine Mercy chants lingered throughout.

"Heather, look what I found in the lotus that withered in the morning! The emerald stone that was missing from the Chalice!", Eleven, the green frog with yellow eyes, cried.

Her identical twin, Heather, leaped on to the banks of Mageia, the river. Mageia was dappled with lotus pads and blooms. Heather and Eleven spent most of their time over there, occasionally squatting on its bank and taking a round in the Golden Chamber.

"Eleven, I am sure it's the doing of Ace. He would have hidden the gems stolen from the chalice inside the lotus bloom. Did you notice the headband of Asura, the robot? It was speckled with precious stones. Let's inform Master Patrick about this swindling."

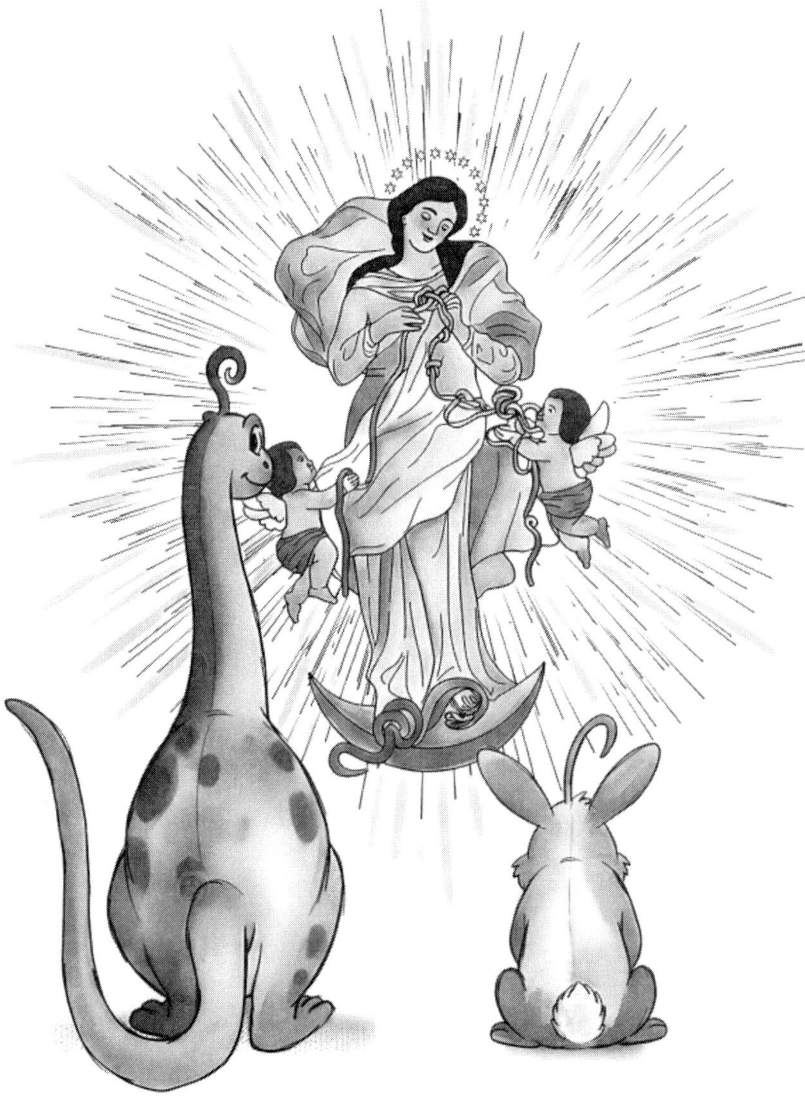

Hand in hand, Heather and Eleven ambled along the river bank, heading towards the Shemrock tree.

Every Saturday, a beautiful lady appeared in the sky with a long thread, full of knots. Two angels who stood on either side of her, tried to help the lady with undoing the knots. The mystical image of the pretty lady almost blinded the eyes of the onlookers. The apparition was accompanied by a beautiful melody- "Ave.. Ave.. Ave Maria!!"

"Ave Maria, Gratia Plena,
Dominus tecum,
Benedicta tu in mulieribus, et benedictus
fructus ventris tui, lesus!"

"Sancta Maria, Mater Dei,
Ora pro nobis peccatoribus, nunc et in
hora mortis nostrae. Amen."

Ethos and Easter pleaded to the most beautiful virgin in the sky earnestly for curing the blind Ace. They offered white roses to her and the lady descended upon the golden chamber, entering the SacroSanctum. Ace was denied access to it ever since he ate the Forbidden fruit. Ethos had made duplicate E kutty keys, the one in the possession of Ace which was earlier distorted to an M shape, has taken the shape of W now.

Ethos and Easter spent most of their time in the Sacrosanctum, which resembled a grotto shaped like a brain. Ace's distorted key would never fit into the keyhole of Sacrosanctum. The roof was open, tears trickled down the eyes of both the siblings when they witnessed the apparition of Mother Mary.

The beautiful virgin wasn't alone when she descended to the

Sacrosanctum. On her shoulders sat a white female dove. Her hands held a white male lamb. Yes, Mother of God was only obeying the commands of God, the mother or the Holy Spirit and Her Son Jesus Christ , the Lamb. Ethos and Easter prostrated before them with their pregnant bellies as Ace began to knock the door with heavy thuds.

"Little Master, let me help you with this", Saying so, Asura tried to insert the key in the keyhole. The distorted key broke into two pieces - V and V. They flew and clung to Ace's 'L' horn.

"What have you done you nincompoop! " before Ace vented his anger upon him, Asura dodged smartly and fled the scene.

"Her fingers are slender and there is no knot that wouldn't open into them."

Chapter 12

God, the Mother

" Mothers two we have,
Resting on heaven above,
All splendour and glory are theirs,
Now, then and forever,
To Father, the Son and the Mother,
May all knees bend in fervour."

Ace was panting after a prolonged gallop towards Mageia. "Cool mate, cool!" Hiss came out of a sound sleep in the depths of the cozy hole in the old trunk of the wild fig tree.

"What makes you run so fast in spite of your blocked vision?" Hiss asked him, pandiculating and slowly creeping along the broad shoulders of the mighty horse.

Ace's anger seemed to melt away into thin air as she crawled across his chest and passionately wound herself to his L horn, now flanked by the 2 V's . Hiss's body made a perfect knot around the red hot L and they were lost in each other once again under the cursed tree.

"Ah, my sweetheart. You are the only balm to my wounds" mumbled the mighty one to the earthy one as they copulated. "Only

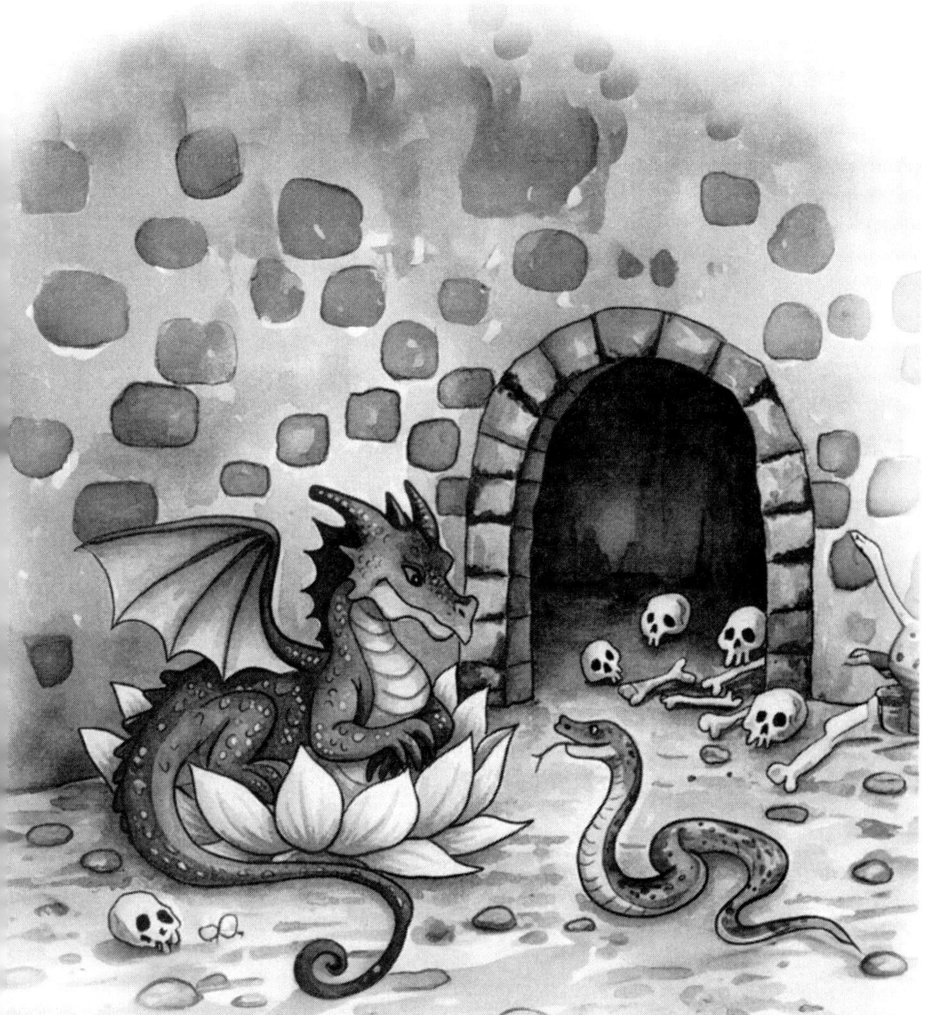

if I could behold your seductive body! " Exclaimed the blind animal.

"You would soon be out of this mess, my love. I promise.. Don't you trust me?" Hiss only winked at the old dragon as she unwound herself from the handsome hunk.

"Let that day come soon". Saying this, Ace trotted away aimlessly. Hiss watched him go. She crept stealthily towards a burrow beneath the Willow tree in Half land.

"Well done my sweet daughter... How dare that old fool Patrick try to pluck off the carefully planted L horn from the bosom of his idiot offspring. You are the rightful heir to this kingdom of wickedness. Ha ha ..." chuckled the old dragon couching on the receptacle of a huge red Lotus flower. It was all muddy waters beneath the burrow. With its obnoxious stench of drains of human blood and carcasses, the under-world of Half land was a stark contradiction to the atmosphere of the golden chamber.

"Yes my beloved Father, You are the King of this whole world". Reciprocated Hiss, bowing low to the Emperor of the world beneath. "But I fear this lady, my dear Father..." He looked at her inquisitively.

"Oh! She descended there,finally? That which I always dreaded! Those stupid Dino and rabbit. I should have seen this coming", pondered the ancient beast.

"I endow you, my darling daughter, with all my powers gathered from the ancient times. You are my true successor, the only one who can get the son to kill his own father, before the whole lot gets their way to the Grand Ocean, the world denied to us, the rightful owners of it." The dragon spewed blazing tongues of fire that even took Hiss by surprise.

"Yes Father. Here I go.Wish me good luck". Hiss bowed once again to the wicked beast before leaving the old cursed chamber under the Weeping Willow tree.

Ace had stumbled upon the door of the Sacrosanctum and heard the "Ave Maria" chants. He could feel the presence of the Lady, the Lamb and the Spirit. Ace never regretted eating the Forbidden fruit for he couldn't fathom the fact that the touch of Grace was blocked due to his disobedience to Patrick.

Ace felt that he rightly deserved to be inside the Sacrosanctum and Patrick was being partial towards his siblings. The fact that three special guests were inside the Sacrosanctum denying him access was an even more bitter pill to swallow.

The Dove flew from the Sacrosanctum and perched on its door and gazed at Ace. Ace was standing on his hind legs about to charge. The Dove pecked at his eyes and Ace groaned in pain. A beautiful lady in white attire stood in the place of Dove. It was none other than God, the Mother commonly addressed as the Holy Spirit. Her head resembled that of a White Dove, while her body resembled that of a beautiful woman. The apparition spread an aura of absolute grace.

"Why do you torment me all the more? Who are you? Why am I denied access to the Sacrosanctum?" Ace's voice choked as he had no strength to speak further.

"You do not deserve to be here in the first place. Ethos and Easter earnestly pleaded with me for your entry to the Golden Chamber. I am God, the Mother. How can a mom ignore the pleas of her kids? And what did you do conspiring with Hiss? Your siblings will never stop interceding for you even now! Ethos finds it hard to squeeze through the door of sacrosanctum with his pregnant belly, yet he does that willingly for your salvation! Easter fasts on two days a week only for Grace from the above to descend on you! I am a merciful mother who wishes all her offspring to be redeemed for eternity. I am the abode of peace who gives umpteen chances to them until they turn to me and remain in GRACE forever."

Ace was alarmed at this new revelation. A sense of shame and remorse overpowered him and he trotted away from the place like a flash of lightning.

Patrick saw Ace as he galloped away to the mystical river. Ace came to a halt and drank the crystalline water. His heavily pregnant belly was now visibly protruding.

"Six more months before the triplets will be born!"

Patrick saw the blinding image of God, the Mother in front of him, holding a malnourished, brown puppy in her arms. He prostrated before her and cried.

"Eunice, my baby! Forgive your Papa for not being available to you when you were in dire need of me." Patrick ran after the puppy who had alighted from God the Mother's hands and scampered away.

Rafa, the Moroccan shepherd was on the lookout for the lamb that had strayed away from his flock.

"Hello croakers! Have you seen a white lamb loitering along the banks? I fear for the life of my little one who had drifted away from me while I took my flock to the river. God the Mother wiped my tears and guided me to this place, the Golden Chamber."

Heather and Eleven looked at each other and pointed to the Shemrock tree. There sat Master Patrick, fondling the missing lamb on his lap.

"Nice to meet you, young boy! We live on the banks of Mageia. Come with us and meet our master. We heard the bleating of a lamb early in the morning and was wondering about its source. Don't worry, your lamb is in the safest hands. Ribbit !! Ribbit !!" The frogs croaked in unison.

"Is Her beauty more radiant or Her wisdom more beautiful; but She always existed!"

Chapter 13

The Love Triangle

" Premarital Virginity is both a covetable virtue and a valuable adornment for a maiden. Eternal vigilance is the only safeguard."

"Mavis, When did you come?" Sierra's pale face further lost its sheen at the sight of him reclining in her living room sofa.

"Half an hour back. Aamal opened the door for me and told that you were taking a shower upstairs. He said he was learning his prayers for the Holy Communion preparation. Is Mahesh not home yet?"

"I have told you a zillion times that I do not wish to see your face. Each time I try to forget that cursed moment, you turn up at my doorstep. Will you stop visiting me for God's sake?" Sierra broke down, tears streaming down her countenance.

"Sierra, tell me the truth. Do you really love Mahesh? What makes him more acceptable to you than me? I haven't forgotten you even after these twelve years. I can't imagine somebody lying by my side other than you, dear Sierra. Why don't you understand me?"

Mavis heard Mahesh's car getting parked at the porch. He got up quickly and left the place instantly.

"Saw Mavis going out just now. Why didn't you ask him to stay for a while? "

"He was about to leave. I told him to wait for you. What took you so long?" Sierra turned and began to fiddle with a coaster. She didn't want Mahesh to catch her eyes disclosing a lie.

"He wants you to sing for the album we are producing. We are in our final round of talks with the Director of the recording studio. The deal will be finalised this Friday. Sierra, please sing for my sake. You can't just waste your talents and confine yourself within the four walls of this house."

Sierra had started to fiddle with a paper weight while Mahesh was talking. It fell and broke into pieces, scattering the shards of glass. What she heard just then was indigestible. The images of her good old days singing alongside Mavis flashed before her eyes and she fell on the sofa, exhausted like never before. Reliving those blissful moments seemed more like a torture now.

"Sierra, Are you ok? You almost broke your dainty fingers!" Mahesh took her palm, kissing it softly.

Sierra, Mavis and Mahesh were classmates, doing Psychology stream for graduation in College. Mavis was Sierra's second cousin. They both became very close when they joined the Music Club. Sierra was the lead singer while Mavis played the guitar. Within no time, they both fell deeply in love. The lovebirds frequented the college canteen, bunked the classes to watch movies and stroll on the beach.

It was a smooth sailing for the couple- the besotted lovers oared happily to the shores of dalliance until the third link of the love triangle came into the picture. Mahesh was instantly drawn to Sierra when he heard her sing for the first time. Though he came from a pretty well-off family, he couldn't resist the lure of money when he learnt that Sierra was the only girl of Tony, the wealthy Squadron leader and Grace, the General Manager of the Lotus Bank.

Sierra and Mavis broke up one fine day, gaining Mahesh's entry to her heart. Sierra had a strict uncompromising policy on premarital virginity which Mavis tried to breach in an unguarded moment when only both were left in the college after the song rehearsals. Mavis groped her from behind, took her unawares. Sierra tried to free herself from his clutches. The blind masculine might at last, overpowered her. Sierra felt lost and disillusioned and would never forgive Mavis for robbing the sacred virginity against her will.

"Love is light, ready for a flight and never smothers with its weight."

Chapter 14

The Malady called Depression!

"It's raw, it's real and is abnormally normal."

Tony wanted to invite a special guest for Aamal's Holy Communion. He took an invitation card from the bundle and addressed the envelope:

To
Dr Sita Mridula,
14/78, Melody Park Inn,
Mother's Street,
Devanahalli,
Bangalore North.

A week after, Tony's email notification chimed on his mobile.

Dear Dad,

It was a moment of great pleasure and pride for me. Mom had told me years back that I was born in Darjeeling. The day she disclosed the identity of my father, I wept bitterly. It was too much for an eighteen year old to take. And yes, it was a solace for me to know that I was conceived with so much love by a handsome pilot

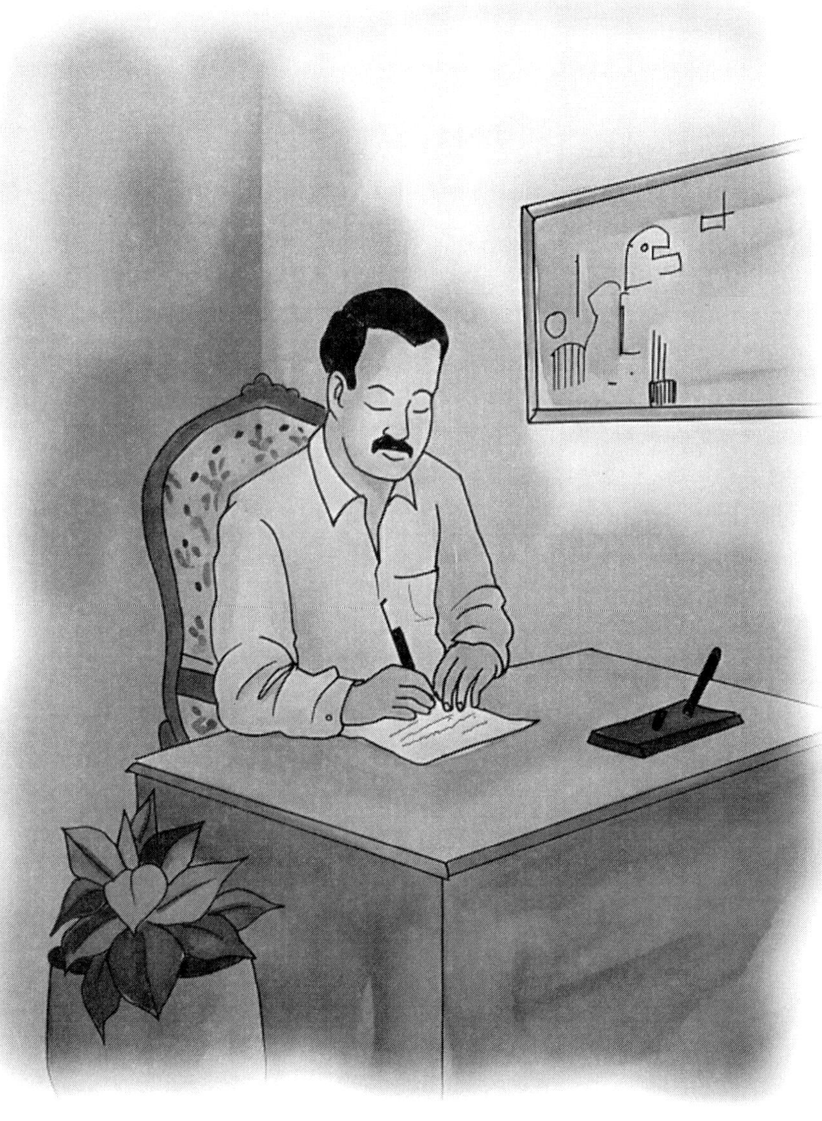

and a beautiful airhostess in the pristine valley that overlooked the hills of Gangtok . She always spoke high of you. When mom got afflicted with Cancer, she didn't want to bother you and disrupt your happy married life. When she breathed her last in April, 2019, I didn't shed a drop of tear for her- I know she is in that distant land, free from pain and suffering. I feel she is constantly by my side, unwilling to part from me for even a second.

A train of memories raced through Tony's mind- his pilot training years in the foothills of Darjeeling, falling in love with the charismatic airhostess trainee Mridula and their frequent trips to Gangtok on weekends. The morning mist of those enchanting hills shrouded the sexagenarian's longing eyes. Wiping a lone teardrop from the corner of his eye, Tony opened his chest of drawers. There lay correspondences from Mridula dated till March, 2000. Tony's welled-up eyes scanned through those letters once more. Mridula called him Chekov, as Tony's name reminded her of the great Russian playwright and short story writer whose fan she was, Anton Chekov. He retrieved an email from Mridula, dated April, 2019.

Dear Chekov,

How are you? Sorry to bother you after these prolonged years. My days are numbered, I have been diagnosed with Blood Cancer. Our daughter Sita is a doctor now. I don't want her to live the life of an orphan when I bid farewell to this world. Hope everything is well at your end. I know that you are leading a blissful married life which I always dreamt of for us.. But certain things are bound to happen in life and the whole Universe might conspire against your happiness.

I have only one request, Chekov. Do accept our daughter and give her all the love that is rightfully due to her from a father.

Yours,

Mridu.

Dr Sita is a leading psychiatrist now. Tony has been suffering from depression for many years. It mainly arose from his feelings of guilt- of hiding the secret of Mridula and Sita from Grace. He loved his wife and kids, but a part of his conscious mind always yearned for Mridula whom he had to ditch with a heavy heart while she was already carrying Sita. The loss of Tony and Grace's first child only added salt to the pestering wound. Tony was guilt-stricken. Why was God punishing his newborn, a baby girl, for a mistake her dad committed in his bachelor days? It took months for him to recover from the unexpected loss of his daughter in her sleep due to Sudden Infant Death Syndrome. To overcome his insomnia, Tony started taking sleeping pills, the overdose of which led to his treatment of depression.

"Grace, Is Tony ok? Heard that he is under treatment for depression. What could be the reason though? You both lead a happy life .Tony often says that you are a blessing in his life. Looks like he hasn't shared the secrets of the dark corners of his heart even to you, but me alone. I can't rid this of my mind. What would bother him so much to the point of attempting to take his life?" Tony's colleague and confidante Mathew had rung up Grace one day.

Tony was reluctant to take the prescribed tablets as they made his mouth dry. Once he felt he was ok, he discarded the tablets altogether. The antidepressants made him drowsy which was reason enough for the tablets to be ditched. It was the common mistake most patients suffering from depression committed, which only made matters worse. Your tranquility gets traded for greater pitfalls of depression in the future and even heavier doses eventually line up your medical list.

A sharp, stabbing pain engulfed Tony's chest, his mind unable to bear the weight of the dark secret- a secret which could possibly put him in trouble.

Tony saw Sita for the first time when Grace was still alive. It was Lotus Bank's Golden Jubilee Celebrations. Grace was working as a Senior Executive to the Southern Zone of Lotus Bank, headquartered at Bengaluru. The grand Jubilee function was inaugurated by none other than Sri Sri Mahishacharya, the founder of the Elixir of life. Pindrop silence was broken by chants of Great life! Great life! from the awestruck audience who listened with rapt attention to the self-styled Guru with tips of Life mantras.

In the front row sat Grace, Tony, Sierra and Solomon. "Isn't he just mind blowing, Sita?" exclaimed Sierra to her close friend and the would-be Psychiatrist at KIMHANS. Sita smiled knowingly, which neither said Yes nor No. Dr Sita was on the Bank's panel for mental health and wellbeing of Lotus Bank staff, specially brought on special deputation by Grace as she heard a lot about the leading Psychiatrist from Sierra.

“Gracias Senora”... Dr Sita was a bit taken aback as Tony greeted her while proceeding for dinner, expecting a hand shake. Well dressed in his Navy blue blazer and perfectly ironed trousers and a pristine white shirt, he still looked smart in his late fifties. Sita reluctantly shook her hands with him, he looking at her with a sparkle in his eyes as if meeting a long lost friend. “Papa, this is my dearest friend Sita”, introduced Sierra, giggling as usual.

“Please come over to our home some day for dinner.” Grace didn't forget to invite Sita to her luxurious recently constructed bungalow. “Don't forget to bring your family along” added Tony, still looking into her eyes. Sita just smiled.. “It's me and me alone in my family.” It was a hard truth she had come to terms with off late.

As the day wound up, in the bedroom upstairs, Solomon’s hands began to tremble, his heart was pounding and he sweated profusely.

Chills and hot flashes overpowered him. He felt dizzy, his vision was blurred and the impending doom made him lose control. He fell to his bed, having lost the race, like very many youngsters of his age. His phone notification beeped for it had picked up a newly released porn video for its regular customer.

The malady called depression stings you from within, its pug marks always deftly hidden from outside. No escape from its clutches- the tentacles of the Octopus are sure to squeeze you hard and suck the life out of you sooner or later.

" My light is lost, memories haunt me and they say your mind needs rest"

Chapter 15

Mystical River - The Witness

"She winds through hills and valleys chronicling the past, quenching her ultimate thirst, once for all, in the bottomless Ocean."

"Master, We see that the lamb on your lap doesn't belong to the Golden Chamber. Meet Rafa, the Moroccan shepherd who is here in search of his lost lamb. " Eleven, the frog, gestured to Rafa.

"You are right. She doesn't belong here. Rafa.. that's your name, right? What brings you to the Golden Chamber? Have you, by any chance, met an emaciated brown puppy who has probably not eaten for days together? Patrick looked at Rafa with quizzical eyes. The lamb sprang up at the sight of Rafa and he lifted the lamb. Nestling her close to his chest, Rafa retorted,

"Master Patrick, this is my lamb who got strayed away from my flock. Mageia guided me to this place. Yes, on my way here, I was blessed to meet God the Mother and Eunice, the puppy."

"Come on, honeybunch, let me take you on a tour around the Golden Chamber." It was Asura, the robot offering his hands to the lamb. Though his limbs were mechanised, his charming face was strikingly human. The lamb had the best time of his life as Asura took her to a meadow and played 'hide and seek' with him. Asura treated her and Rafa with Irish delicacies and truffle chocolates. Ferrying them to Mageia, he waved them goodbye.

Mageia, the mystical river in the golden chamber has witnessed very many things and is an indispensable link in the history of Patrick and his protégé. Patrick met Isabella, the doe-eyed beauty, on the banks of Mageia when she had drifted from her hometown to quench her insatiable thirst. She lived in the Half Land, a mystical place which was neither up in the sky nor down on the land. It was love at first sight for both of them. Their union was solemnized by God, the Mother and the Mother of God.

They engaged themselves in acts of love several times and Isabella gave birth to Ethos, Easter and Ace within a span of three years. She passed away during childbirth, the labour lasting for almost three days. On the second day of her labour, it became known to her that Patrick cheated by making love with Helen, the dusky lass, who was also her best friend in the Half Land.

After Ethos was born, Patrick had visited the Half Land to inform Isabella's kith and kin about the baby. During his brief stay, he met the gorgeous Helen who was the cynosure of all young men. He was lured by her beauty and Helen too reciprocated his feelings. Patrick was as fit as a fiddle, he was the most handsome man she had ever met. They had consummated their love before parting ways.

Helen gave birth to Eunice, the puppy, after six months. Patrick was informed of her birth through Mageia, but he never acknowledged them. A deep sense of guilt overpowered him.

"I shouldn't have cheated Isabella.. that too with her best friend. I can't even acknowledge Helen and our child." Patrick never set his foot upon Half Land since then.

"Eunice, my baby, forgive me for everything I have done to you and Helen. I have lost them both - Isabella and Helen. Come with me, I'll introduce you to your siblings." Patrick held her by the hand and next took her to the Sacrosanctum where the pregnant Ethos

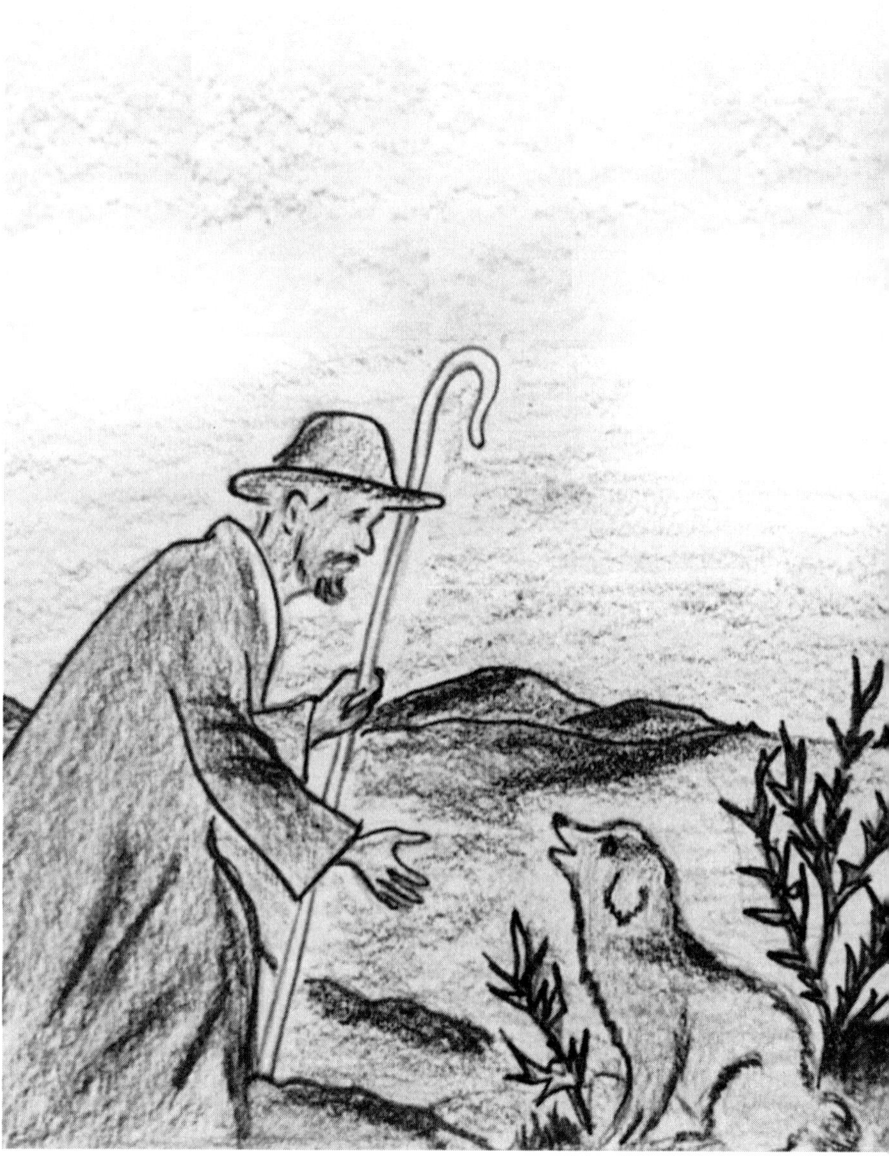

and Easter spent most of their time.

"Do you know my mom, Master Patrick? She never told me who my dad was. She said my dad was a great man and I have three siblings from another mom. When she passed away in her sleep, people of Half Land didn't know what to do with me. Mageia carried me on her back and brought me here."

"Master, who is she? Why does she resemble us?" Ethos scanned the puppy's face with his tongue which was longer than his spiky tail.

"She is Eunice, your sister from another mom. She has lost her mom , just like you have lost yours. She will stay with us in the Golden Chamber hence forth ." Ethos and Easter hugged and patted her on the back.

Eunice was next led to Ace, who showed no interest in accommodating another inmate in the Golden Chamber. When Patrick told him that Eunice was his sister, he turned the other way.

"I don't want The Golden Chamber to be divided among one more person, no matter if she is my so-called 'sister'." Ace clearly showed his displeasure by snorting as he galloped away from the scene.

"As if what he has stolen isn't enough!", Heather, the frog sneered at Ace.

"Master Patrick, Ace has stolen some of your precious stones from the Sacrosanctum. We found one of his spoils inside the lotus bud this morning." Eleven handed over the emerald stone to the master. Patrick examined the stone and headed towards Mageia that cut through rocks and pebbles, flowing to the majestic Grand Ocean on the other side of the Golden Chamber.

"A river is a witness to births and rebirths, its water always pure; refreshing hearts weary of dirts."

Chapter 16

Grand Ocean- Grandeur in Gold

"The river bride met her ocean groom, her flowy veil carefully lifted by him as she was led to the nuptial chamber."

Patrick sat meditatively alongside the shores of Mageia. He looked at his reflection in the crystalline waters.

"You have grown old, my darling!"

He came out of the tranquil water bed as Mageia extended her silvery arms to pat the hairy cheeks of the Master of Golden chamber.

A lovely hymn chimed from afar:

"Irukaratharil...sweekarikkoo."

" The Golden chamber's sweet music has crossed past you, dear Mageia!" Patrick's eyes twinkled as they searched for the source.

"Well, that's my boy, who never ceased singing the glory of the Grand Ocean ever since he came to my lap as a suckling infant", declared Mageia, like any proud mother.

Patrick watched the teen collect lilac flowers from the river bed. His tunic was ornamental with golden inscriptions of a lamb carrying a cross in the front and a golden chalice alongside grapes on the rear of his vestment. The tunic fluttered in the breeze, yet it completely covered his slender figure.

Fides, Filo and Fina were the guardian nymphs of the Golden Chamber. They belonged to the Grand Ocean. Fina resembled a mermaid nymph. Fides and Filo looked like a lark and a nightingale nymph respectively.

"Fina, How has Ace turned blind all of a sudden? He is creating such a ruckus in the Golden Chamber. Can't you do something about it?" Fides voiced her concern.

"Well, that's because he ate the forbidden fruit. Before I could warn him, he got trapped by Hiss. The only antidote for his blindness is to fetch the magic coral reef from the Grand Ocean." Fina answered in the affirmative.

"Easter was very much concerned about Ace. She told me that Ethos and herself were planning to do fasting for him. They believe that Patrick will forgive Ace for his disobedience and cure him of his blindness. I strictly forbade them from doing so, as they are carrying triplets and will be risky to do so now." Filo crooned.

"Let's ask Mageia to bring the coral reef from the Grand Ocean. We are on duty now, we can't leave them alone here." Filo and Fina nodded at Fides' suggestion.

The bird nymphs and the fish nymph approached Mageia with their request. Mageia splashed some water and the crystalline water droplets fell on the nymphs and shone in the sun. Mageia began her voyage to collect the magical coral reef from the Grand Ocean.

The Grand Ocean was a marvellous sight to behold. Its waves were lustrous, giving a regal appearance. As Mageia approached the amber-coloured coral reef in the backdrop of the aurelian Grand ocean, she was stopped by a water snake. It hissed and spewed venom at Mageia. It was none other than Hiss, Ace's bestie and love interest. Mageia was very agile and dodged effectively. Hiss slithered behind, shifting her shape to that of the Leviathan, the monster serpent.

" Stop there, you filthy river! How dare you snatch the coral reef treasured for years by my Master? I won't let you get away just like that." Hiss wound around Mageia and fumed.

The Master she was referring to was none other than the Dragon, who was trying to usurp the realm of the Grand Ocean. Mageia freed herself from the clutches of the serpent, trampling it under her majestic feet.

The Dragon's persistent snarls were heard from the ocean bed. Wasting no time, Mageia gushed forth towards the Golden Chamber with the coral reef tightly secured against her bosom.

"All the ways, however diverse they appear, are always bound for the same Grand Ocean, its golden waves sparkling glitter."

Chapter 17

The Crossword Puzzle

"Life throws you clues, the one who takes the hints wisely cracks the puzzle in no time!"

"Abba, Could you help me with this crossword puzzle clue? I need to get only one more answer to solve this." Fatima, the 11 year old, was in high spirits.

"Ok, let me have a look at it. Promise me, you will do your Maths Homework after this." Ibrahim fondled his daughter's lovely, long, ebony black tresses.

"Clue No:7

Faithfulness to a person, cause, or belief, demonstrated by continuing loyalty and support.

It's an eight letter word. What's the answer, Abba?" Fatima had pinned her ultimate hope on Ibrahim.

"Oh, that's easy- It's FIDELITY."

"Abba, You are a genius!" Fatima solved the puzzle instantly and started doing her homework.

Ibrahim looked at their family photo and sighed. Fatima looked so cheerful in the snap. She was flanked by her parents, Ibrahim and Delilah. The photograph clicked at the pristine valley was from the trip they had made to Kulu Manali the previous year.

"How happy we were! How did our joyful world fall upside down all of a sudden? Who cast an evil eye on us? I still love you Delilah.. Had you picked up my call for once! I have already forgiven you, I can't wait anymore to see you. When you turn up at my doorstep, I shall passionately welcome you."

Ibrahim reminisced that fateful night as he tucked Fatima in bed.

"Delilah, What's this? Fatima has failed again in all her subjects! When her teacher called me to go through her report card, I was taken aback! Day by day, her marks are getting down and now, she has hit rock bottom. I wonder what you were doing all this time? If I were here, definitely this wouldn't have happened!" Ibrahim pointed his finger accusingly at her.

"What do you expect of me? Isn't she old enough to study by herself? I haven't slept for days ever since I was posted to this new branch. By the time I am back from work, she is sound asleep. You can't blame me just like that!" Delilah raised her voice.

"Fatima is just 11, mind you! She comes daily to a home, with no one to wait upon. Why didn't you call and check on her daily? Is it too hard for a busy mom? It's as if she were your last priority. You care only about your prospects and nothing else. How did you stoop so low, Delilah? You weren't like this earlier!" Ibrahim couldn't control his words.

That was it.. the last nail on the coffin. Months of pent up frustration on being forced to be a 'single parent' has to be released one day. Delilah packed her bags and walked away as the dawn broke.

"Solomon, I am afraid I am pregnant. The pregnancy strip showed two faint lines." Delilah's trembling voice seemed like a death knell to Solomon.

"O Shit! How did those stupid condoms go wrong? We can't

have this baby at any cost. Fix an appointment with a gynaec and get it terminated at the earliest." A year later, Delilah found herself on the crossroads of motherhood again.

Delilah had come back after visiting Fatima on her birthday. She met Ibrahim and something unusual tugged at her heartstrings as he extended his hands to her.

"He is still so mad in love with me. They all miss me so much! What have I done? "

The unsolved crossword puzzle sheet lay on the bedside table- Fatima's latest obsession! Delilah had gifted her a coveted book of Crossword Puzzles on her twelfth birthday. Delilah felt nauseated and threw up in the washroom. She had missed her periods for ten days in a row.

"I don't think I can undo the knot I have tied! This puzzle won't be solved anytime soon." Delilah sighed. She couldn't look into their pleading eyes as she quickly bade goodbye to Fatima and Ibrahim.

"I love you, the knave loudly proclaims. I can wait, says the loved one expectantly."

Chapter 18

Unheard Melodies

"Hark! Don't the unheard melodies sound so familiar? "

Aamal's First Holy Communion was a grand event jointly hosted by Tony and Mahesh. The orchestra singers enthralled the guests and the chants "Once more" reverberated across the majestic party hall.

"Good evening, Ladies and Gentlemen,

A warm welcome to one and all gathered here. On this auspicious day, I would like to introduce a special guest to you all. It's none other than Dr Sita, my talented daughter . Give her a big round of applause." Dr. Sita was dumbstruck when she heard the announcement. All eyes turned towards the leading young psychiatrist of the town.

The guests spoke in muffled voices as Sita was conducted to the stage by Sierra. Solomon raised his eyebrows :

"Why was I kept in the dark about all these developments? "

In reality, Solomon had known about his father's illegitimate child, his half-sister, from his late mom. He, along with his mom, would never forget nor forgive Tony for this grave act. Grace, the TB patient, died of pneumonia during her pilgrimage. Had she already forgiven Tony and accepted Sita as her daughter? You will never know as she breathed her last while on the ventilator, with no one by her side.

"Hey hero, Had your food? Here, let me help you with the ice cream bowl. It's your favourite strawberry flavour by the way! " Solomon scooped a dollop of ice cream for Aamal.

Aamal had taken a newfound fancy for the strawberry flavour. What no one knew was, he had stealthily taken a puff or two of his uncle's strawberry flavoured vape. Before he even knew, he was addicted to it. He took it to the school and vaped in the corridors of the wash room along with his friends. He traded the vape for their pocket money and amassed more stock of vape solutions to use in the future.

Maria and family had turned up for Aamal's function. They had all met in Winnie's house after the convocation ceremony of Veer. Maria and the kids had stopped receiving melodies in their dreams by then. They had almost forgotten about it and brushed them away as mere coincidences. Willy was busy signing autographs, for he was by now a well- established writer.

It was exactly 3 years back that Sita realized who her father was. Grace had hosted a lunch for Sita at her beautiful home shortly after the Golden Jubilee celebrations of Lotus Bank. Tony was astonished to know that Sita was all alone in this world and it didn't take him long to realise who the beautiful girl from Darjeeling was, with the same dreamy eyes of Mridula.

The orchestra began to play the unheard melody of "Irukarathaaril" all of a sudden. The lyrics of the song mentioned about the Holy Eucharist and the Mass being offered, turning bread and wine into flesh and blood of Jesus. It was befitting the function, but none of the guests had ever heard it played in the churches for a long time. Maria and the kids couldn't comprehend what their ears had just listened to.. The unheard melodies weren't unheard to them after all!

All felt tired after the prolonged discussions of the day about the reassuring company of each other spread a gleam of contentment in their hearts for a lifetime. Aamal listened carefully to his newfound loving aunty Sita and watched how his mom warmed up to her sisterly endearments. Sierra could feel the love of Grace seeping in through Sita's eyes and enveloping her like a newborn being wrapped up in swaddle after a refreshing bath.

Aamal was tired too. The excitement of his First Holy Communion, the grand celebration followed by the surprise announcement by his grandpa.. Too much excitement for a day. He was soon tucked in bed by Sierra as she placed a warm kiss on his forehead, Sita watching them from the door. His eyes closed in no time and he delved into a deep slumber.

Aamal opened his eyes to find himself in a yacht, sailing through silvery waters. At the helm of the yacht sat a handsome man in his fifties, with a golden French beard, his eyes fixated at something afar. Aamal made a move towards him as he noticed a cute little bunny sleeping peacefully on the man's lap.

"Caught you!" Aamal turned around to see the source of a giggle. He was astonished to watch the most unexpected scene. A Dino and a horse playing hide and seek in the yacht!

"Better luck next time. It's your turn my mate" The denner, surprisingly a Snake, emerged from a closet at the corner marked 'Remorse' in bold, handing over the denning wand to the horse. They were all having so much fun together. "Oh come on, I have searched enough all my life and found my dear Dino bro waiting to hug me"... remarked horse. Dino gave them both a big hug, a tear emerging out of the corner of his eyes.

Aamal noticed something in common for all the animals in the yacht. They all bore some scars on their head, something reminding of some horns that existed there earlier. And yet another aspect- all were at absolute peace. A great tranquillity prevailed in the entire yacht. It had a huge flag written GRACE in golden letters, which fluttered in the cool breeze. No one was in a hurry. But everyone's excitement was palpable- as if they were nearing their ultimate destination.

"This song always rings along; lucky are those who have ears to hear."

Chapter 19

Conscience Pricks!

"Pricks of conscience make you bleed, but will never harm you. The red makes you pause and reflect before taking the significant step."

Rafa, the Moroccan shepherd, appeared in Willy's dream that night. He saw the flute grow big in size, to gigantic proportions. It soon occupied the whole room where Willy was sleeping. The melody was out of tune and the doorbell rang once again.

It was Valli who looked visibly upset. Willy and Pauly rushed to the hospital where Vicky was admitted. They learnt from Valli that Vicky had jumped from the eleventh floor of the high rise on which they lived. The chances of his survival were narrow as his spine was badly damaged in the fall, the surgeon informed them.

Prayers were chanted by Vicky's kith and kin, anxiously waiting in the hospital corridors. Valli leaned her head on Maria's shoulders, who knew the feelings best when your loved one is operated upon.

"She should have given us a hint about Victor's mental state. We could have found a way out to combat his depression."

"He never gave us any hint of what he was going through."

"Heard that he was under medication for so many years. He

should have quit his job. It's too much pressure in the IT sector."

The blame game was going on, whispers were heard, various suggestions were made, but the door of the operation theatre remained closed.

Mageia handed over the coral reef to Fina, the physician nymph. Ace was nowhere to be seen. Ethos and Easter along with Fides and Filo wandered outside the Golden chamber.

"You should know Ace, Patrick is the biggest hurdle in your path to glory." Hiss whispered in Ace's ears.The sense of hearing was sharp now in Ace because of his blindness. The scene of crime where the plotting happened was in a valley adjacent to the Golden chamber. There were no inhabitants there, except the scavenger birds who tore open the dead bodies of doomed people on earth.

Hiss lived there and Ace had met her when he strayed away from the Golden chamber once after midnight.

She took out a luminous stone from her head and handed it over to Ace.

"Here, take this stone with you. It will make you doubly powerful and guide you correctly to Patrick. He will be sleeping under the Shemrock tree now. You have to charge at him and pierce his chest with your horn. Just imagine, the Golden chamber will all be yours in a few moments from now."

Asura helped his master get out from the stinky dungeon of the Dragon who was the masterbrain behind the rebellion against Patrick. Asura took a fascination for the ruby red stone handed by Hiss. He placed the heart-shaped stone on his armoured chest.

"Isn't she so pretty? The maiden is pretty like a wild flower sleeping in the meadows! There is another one in the next street... It's just pretty girls everywhere!" Asura began to play a mesmerizing melody on his bagpipe.

Vamika and her friend Jennifer were up, as if in a trance. They tiptoed in their pajamas and sat by the window side, gazing up at the sky. Asura descended there as a charming young man, gently lifting the maidens and putting them on bed. His golden tresses flew in the night breeze. Undressing the maidens, he kissed them first on their half closed eyelids, then on the neck and further down, on their tender breasts.

"You are so irresistible, young lady! I shall take you to the golden chamber. Let's make love under the Forbidden tree like my master and his beloved. I mean, there is no harm in making out and getting to know each other if you are in love . It's perfectly normal!"

Vamika tossed on her bed, thinking about her boyfriend at the school. The wall clock chimed three times- it was 3 am. Her palpitations rose and she found herself naked on bed.

"Was it a dream? It felt so real.. the enchanting music and that bagpiper!"

Next day at school, her friend Jennifer narrated the same dream episode which she had.

The red light in the shape of a heart blinked outside the theatre.

"Doctor, the patient's heart beat has slowed down", remarked the Head nurse pointing at the monitor.. Dr Amalam, busy so far with the operation, casually looked at the screen. "Oh my, my.. It's a gone case now." Vicky's heart began to pump faster as his eyeballs oscillated beneath the eyelids.

"How did you reach here, Vicky uncle! " Aamal exclaimed, sitting beside the man in the yacht. Vicky was exasperated and felt the stark difference as he got into the yacht sailing peacefully in the serene blue waters.

Vicky looked at the man at the helm with the sleeping bunny in his lap. He felt he was back home. "Get down from your horse. Come, come, let's play hide and seek". Vicky recognized a familiar voice as he turned around to see the Dino, making his most amusing smile.

The bunny opened her eyes and looked around meekly. Her eyes warmed at the sight of the new comers. The sailor caressed her and steered the yacht towards right as they were welcomed to the Grand Ocean by a whole array of larks making a big V in the sky. The melodious song starting "Irukaratharil" by the larks was led by a gorgeous lark with the body of a woman. She flew high in the air as the pristine white laces of her tunic made a beautiful trail in the blue sky.

"The melody that haunted me, is for real!" Vicky exclaimed at the wonderful sight.

"The party has just begun dude!". Vicky and Aamal were taken for a pleasant surprise as a mermaid splashed the golden waters of the Ocean upon them. It did not wet them. Instead, they felt as if touched by a soft feather making a scintillating sensation of childlike glee.

The sky changed its hue from blue to pink and then orange as a group of nightingales joined the larks in another V shape, thus making a perfect W. The "Irukaratharil" melody was heard across the vast expanse of the Ocean as the golden waves twirled and swirled, dancing to the enchanting tune.

"Time for a brisk evening walk". Now who is that? Everyone's attention was grabbed by a golden Nightingale who stood in a gorgeous orange hued dress welcoming them into a meadow beneath the Ocean. They couldn't take their eyes off her golden tresses as she glided along the undulating surface of the Ocean in her golden shoes, accompanied by the She Lark and the Mermaid.

"What a breathtaking spectacle! Look at those purple flowers, Vicky Uncle.. " The excitement in Aamal's voice was understandable. A meadow of flowers of all hues, sizes and textures spread over an unending expanse. A graceful lady, dressed all in white and a white

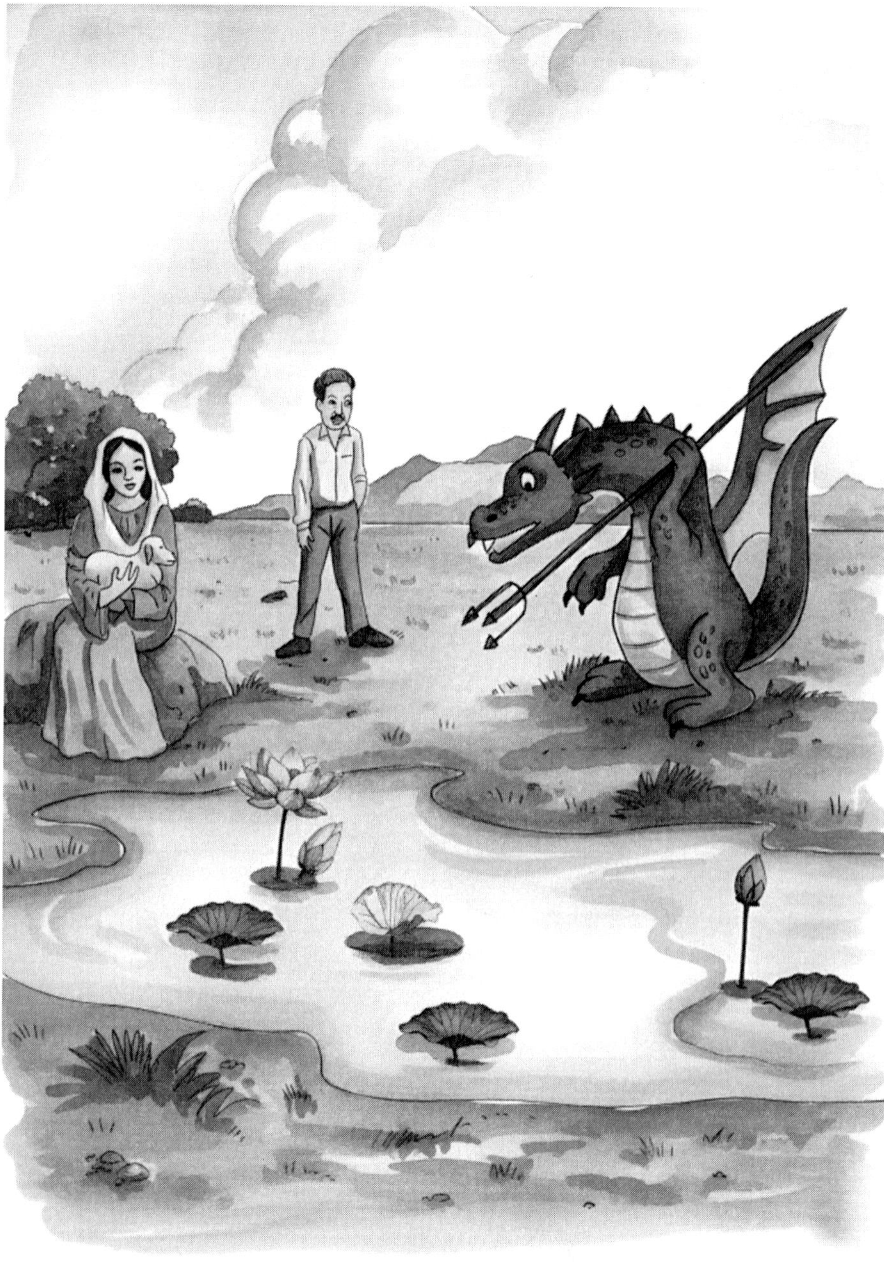

cloak, walked majestically in the meadows followed by a trail of angels happily fluttering their wings wherever She went. And oh! there was this sweet chorus in the background.

Mary had a Little Lamb
Little Lamb, Little Lamb
And wherever that Mary went..
The Lamb was sure to go.

She put the Lamb in Her arms gently on the ground as Her attention was diverted to a Lotus flower bud about to be plucked off by a water monster that looked like a Dragon by a cord with a trident at its end. The dragon hung on his neck a garland of Lotus buds which had all withered except for their stems that bore marks of a chord tightened around them once for all. Vicky was surprised to see the lotus bud the dragon aimed at bowed before the trident cord. He gulped his spit as his Adam's apple moved up and down, watching the whole scene.

The dragon started trembling as the Lady in white approached the lake of lotus buds. Her eyes glared in anger, contrasting her tranquil aura. Vicky watched in surprise, the rabbit and the Dino chanting "Ave Maria" as they crawled on their knees on the beach sand, hand in hand. The sailor stood facing a hut, helpless, raising his hands to the sky in supplication. Mercy, Mercy, Mercy on him. He chanted unceasingly, his prayer taking the shape of musical notes gliding their way through the windows of the hut.

Aamal looked on breathlessly at all that was going on. By the seashore, there was a neatly thatched hut. The hay glistened in the silvery full moon's light. The hut looked no less than a palace by the serene grandeur that emanated from all its corners. Aamal peeped into the hut's tiny window. There was a bright blue light that shone like a diamond. He slowly entered the hut as he was emboldened by the harmony that existed inside.

Aamal gazed amazingly at the beautifully carved wooden furniture inside the hut glowing majestically in the blue light. All of them bore carvings of a meek lamb and a solemn lady. There couldn't be a being that could look meeker than that lamb. And there couldn't be a woman on earth more graceful than her. All the musical notes that came in through the window floated towards the blue light. Aamal searched for its source. There lay an old bearded man, sleeping peacefully, leaning his head against a pillow, with the word Faith, embroidered beautifully on it. The melody notations danced in delight as they all entered inside the blue heart that throbbed in a beautiful rhythm. The old man got up and sat on the wooden bed carved in the shape of the majestic lady's cloak. He gazed at Aamal and patted his bushy hair.

"Who are you, Sir?" Aamal asked in reverence.

"I'm the lucky husband of Her and the proud father of my lamb who takes away the sins of the whole world." The old man pointed at the Lady in white cloak outside.

From nowhere, the bleating of a lamb was heard, chanting "Abba, Abba ! Mercy, Mercy!" The Lady smiled endearingly at the old man and took a goblet of sparkling red wine from the chest of the Lamb and sprinkled on the bud. The dragon just vanished. He was no more to be seen anywhere around.

"It's a Miracle! Never have I seen such a case of come back in my entire career." Dr Amalam exclaimed as the Head Nurse pointed to the monitor where Vicky's heart beat returned to normal.

"Victor is out of danger now. It's a miracle that he suffered no brain injury in the fatal fall. He needs complete rest now for both body and mind. Our psychiatrist Dr Sita will take care of him. She is very good at handling such critical cases."

Sighs of relief were heard from the bystanders. Valliammai and

Maria hugged each other with tears of joy. Joe smiled from the photo Maria carried in her wallet always.

"My hands are not too short to reach for you! Nor am I too deaf to hear your pleas."

Chapter 20

The Mystical Conclusion

"It's a blessing you can keep your dream in your sleep-dreams as real as life, keep you awake!"

Solomon parked his car in front of "Grace Mansion." He and Sierra had just visited Vicky in the hospital, overlooking his rehabilitation. The siblings opened up to each other after a long time.

"What do you have to say about our 'half sister' Dr Sita? Don't you think she is a golddigger? Note the time she has turned up at Aamal's function!" Solomon's voice disclosed the obvious sneer.

"I don't think she is after money. She has no one else in this world except us! It's our duty to support her and welcome her home. I am sure mom would also do the same if she were alive! By the way, I need to ask you something. Heard that you are having an affair with a lady named Delilah who is estranged from her husband. Is this true?" Solomon's face turned pale all of a sudden.

"Grandpa, will you join online chess with me? I am bored like hell! " Aamal pleaded with Tony who was scanning through the emails sent by Grace to his friend Mathew. Yes, Grace knew about Mridula and Sita a month prior to her unfortunate death. In one of those emails, she mentioned how she had accidentally discovered them and how she was unable to forgive Tony for keeping her in the dark.

"Aamal, You should always wear this scapular of Mamma Mary. She will protect you from all dangers. " Tony handed over the scapular which was carelessly thrown on the bed along with Aamal's Holy Communion dress. After one or two rounds of Chess, Tony retired to bed. Aamal took out the Vape to have a puff, but his eyes fell upon the scapular on his neck. Guilt stricken, he discarded the Vape in the dustbin and slept with his grandfather.

It soon turned pitch dark. This made no difference to Ace as he was fully blind by then. The luminous stone began to work its charm and Ace's eyes began to glow in the dark. His brain was now conditioned by avarice. He positioned himself and charged at Patrick who seemed to be in deep slumber.

"Fides, take this sword and cut his horn. Quick!" Upon Fina's instruction, Fides struck at the inverted 'L' horn with the sword, as quick as a lightning bolt. The Sword had the depiction of the Host, the Holy Eucharist.

Patrick awoke from his slumber and took stock of the situation. Ace's chest was bleeding, the place from where the horn was removed. Hiss and Ace fell on their knees, prostrating before their master, Patrick.

"Forgive us, Master, for we have sinned against you."

Patrick hugged them both, rubbing softly at their pregnant bellies that are going to deliver the triplets. God the Mother descended there with Asura, who came back from the lustful dreams of maidens and was holding the horn of his master.

"Asura, throw the corrupted horn away lest it should defile you! Pour the droplet in your Chalice over the wound of Ace." Asura obeyed the commands of God the Mother to the T. The bleeding stopped at once and only the scar shaped like 'G' remained in the place of the horn.

"Grace be unto you and your blessed wombs!"

Aamal and Tony had the same dream- Grace stood with folded hands wearing a brown scapular. She looked so much at peace in the realm where she was. Grace planted a kiss on Aamal's cheeks and patted on his back by pointing to the discarded Vape. Tony looked at her with pleading eyes. Grace smiled at him . Tony felt the weight was finally lifted from his chest. He was so relieved. Aamal put his hands around his grandpa's neck. Tony hugged him tight and they both slept peacefully with a smile lingering on their lips.

"My peace I give you, which no one shall ever snatch away."

Chapter 21

Love is in the Air, Again!

"It's the physical beauty that catches your eyes first, but the inner beauty is what stirs your soul."

"Have you gone crazy, Delilah? We can't have this child at any cost."

"Solomon, I can't stay away from Fatima for long. I love you, but I realize that Ibrahim's heart is where I belong to. I lose my identity when I stray away from his heart. Please let me go back. You know something.. he told me he is ready to accept me even if I am carrying your child." Delilah cried inconsolably.

"I don't think I will ever get over you, Delilah. I love you more than anyone else in this world. But if you get more happiness by leaving me for Ibrahim, I am willing to let you go."

Delilah hugged him for the last time and kissed his forehead.

It was the third anniversary of the publishing of William Joseph's children's novel, "The Mystery of the Golden Chamber." The first and second editions of the bestseller ran out of stock from the book shops in no time. Asura toys were in high demand. Teenagers thronged the online sites and had to queue up for months before the toy was delivered to their doorsteps. The Hatrick truffle chocolates based on the book were a big hit among the kids. The Halloween nights saw youth roam around in Asura costumes and kids' "Trick or treat" baskets laden with Hatrick truffles instead of the traditional candies.

The third edition of the young adult fiction was to be launched on its third anniversary and the occasion called for a grand celebration. The agents of the Shemrock Publication house based in Ireland arranged a success party in Bangalore for its Indian readers. The invitees were mostly young adults from all parts of India who were the winners of the book contest based on the novel. The "Five Eyes" had a reunion of sorts- the cousins graced the event, bringing their friends along. Violet and Veona compered their dad's event. Their cousins Veer and Vaneet entertained the guests with their unique games.

"It's time for the highlight of tonight- the surprise game specially designed for all you wonderful people gathered here. It is time for the "Passing the Patrick" game and guess what? It's conducted by none other, but yours truly, the one and only Asura! Give him a big round of applause."

Vamika walked in, blindfolded with the Asura costume and the Patrick Hat. Asura played songs from the playlist enabled by AI upon demands from the guests. The Patrick Hat had to be worn and passed on to the next. The contestant with the hat on got out of the game when the music stopped . As the rule changes in the end, the winner was the one who remained with the Patrick Hat on. It so happened that Aamal and Jennifer competed in the final round. The music abruptly stopped as the hat was worn by Jennifer.

"Put your hands together for Jennifer, our winner of "Passing the Patrick game." She will receive a special Patrick Hat with lots of goodies from the Golden Chamber!"

Jennifer, the young prodigy, had been declared the winner of the book contest held for young adults from all over India. When "The Mystery of the Golden Chamber" was released, she was the first one to grab a copy of it. Vamika and her friend Jennifer were surprised to find Asura in the novel- the same handsome young man who had visited them in their dreams! How could William, the great writer, visualize the character with such precision?

Jennifer's parents were called to school for a counselling session, for she had begun to show signs of depression. She didn't attend the school, complaining of abdominal pain or chest discomfort. She had panic attacks too at the school. Her parents now spent more time with her and she felt better.

"Jennifer, meet Willy's graceful daughters, Violet and Veona." Vamika introduced her cousins to Jennifer.

"Hey Jennifer, hope to see you after the holidays. We are all waiting for our genius classmate . Vamika said that you have almost finished the manuscript of your debut novel." Vaneet hugged her bestie.

"Thanks dear. I am almost done with the book. I shall be greatly honored to get my book edited by William. It's a meta fiction titled " When the Heavens Chimed!" Jennifer was ecstatic as she spoke about her book to all who had gathered there, especially to Aamal, her newfound love interest. She blushed, as Aamal , the most popular boy of her school congratulated her on the win.

Violet, Veona and Veer, the senior lot, huddled together and talked about their college days. They made a fashion statement with their Golden Chamber- themed outfits which made heads turn. The "Five Eyes" were indeed the cynosure of all eyes!

"Heavens chime in unison when siblings gather in harmony."

Chapter 22

The Reconciliation

"Reconcile with Man, for it's through reconciliation that you become united with the Lord."

It was again dark when Solomon parked his white Jetour at Grace Mansion and hurried upstairs to the shelter of his bedroom."Seems something is seriously wrong" Tony said to himself studying his face as he hurriedly ascended the stairs.

The cries of the baby still echoed in Solomon's ears. "Stop it! For heaven's sake" he muttered, closing his palms tightly over the ears. His heart thumped wildly against the chambers of his chest, his forehead sweating profusely. He quickly took the sleeping pills hidden in his drawer and got into bed in no time.

Next day, Mavis walked in to Solomon's office. "Hey bro! What's the matter with you? You seem to have put on weight in a matter of a month. What's worrying you so much?"

"Im busy right now. We shall meet at the Royal Cheers in the evening."

" Sure." Mavis left the scene, winking at a newly joined female desk officer who offered him a cute smile.

"How could she just forget me like that?" , sobbed Solomon,

after 2 pegs of his favourite Vodka at Royal Cheers.

"And how stupid of that idiot Ibrahim. How does he expect a woman to love him again after she shared her bed with another one! Bro, I will get you your dream girl back. Don't worry".

Solomon looked into Mavis's eyes. " How? What do you mean?"

"Listen to me carefully. You just have to do only one simple thing. Next Sunday, when you go to church, just get a eucharist and accompany me to the place I say, in the midnight. You just have to hand it over to them. That's all. Rest assured, your woman would be back on your toes".

"Caught you! I win this time too.", Heather chuckled as she leaped to the lily pad near Eleven's hiding place. The twin frog sisters felt so much at home in the muddy pond near the sprawling acres of the KIMHANS campus.

Winnie, the Psychology professor, hastened her steps,for it was getting late for the commencement of her lecture. The parking lot was fully occupied and she had to park her car near the muddy pond behind it. Something rustled between the bushes and the faint cry of a baby was heard. Winnie couldn't help but look in that direction. There lay a baby, hardly a few days old swaddled in flannel, discarded in the wilderness. The two frogs took turns as sentries, guarding her from all dangers.

"How do you humans abandon a newborn just like that? Look at her angelic face! Miss, won't you take a closer look?" Eleven pleaded.

A talking frog! Winnie became all the more curious and retraced her steps.

"Ribbit !! Ribbit !! Look, she has a name tag of KIMHANS' maternity ward! Baby Rachel she is! Baby of Delilah Ibrahim." Winnie listened rapturously to Heather's words.

Delilah, carrying Solomon's daughter, had reconciled with her husband. Ibrahim's joy knew no bounds as he welcomed her back along with a jubilant Fatima, eager to rejoin her mom. The father-daughter duo took good care of Delilah, who took the risk of delivering the baby in her middle age. Fatima, the only child, had longed for a sibling for quite some time. She would never leave her mother's side when Delilah complained of cramps or back pain. Ibrahim felt excited to be a dad again, he never differentiated the unborn child from his own biological daughter. Delilah was moved to tears when Ibrahim held Baby Rachel close to his bosom and kissed her gently on the forehead.

"Why was I late to realize your selfless love? I literally cheated on you with Solomon! I don't think I am worthy of your love, Ibrahim!" Delilah broke down.

"What has passed is in the past. You don't have to revisit that and spoil our present. For me, Baby Rachel is an angel who brought us together and helped us rediscover our lost love. She is the light of our present, rekindling our love and the hope of our bright future. Nothing else matters for us." Stroking his wife's hair, Ibrahim handed the baby to Delilah.

Solomon went to the Good Shepherd church for the Sunday Mass earlier than usual. He volunteered to drop Aamal and Sierra too at the church. "Why don't you change to your Tees?" Asked Sierra while serving Idiyappam for breakfast. Tony's eyes welled up as he saw the aromatic fumes emerging from the hotcase as it was opened. Grace made really tasty Idiyappams..And always ensured to make sweetened coconut milk along with it, as she knew that was his favourite combo.

Solomon just shrugged, stealthily peeping into his shirt's pocket. "Yes. It's safe there." He had slipped the eucharist into it with trembling hands. It was soon dark. Everyone retired to their rooms. "Illuminati.. Illuminati"..The hit song from the Malayalam movie

Avesham blasted in a street nearby.

Cu Coo. Cu Coo.. Solomon's cuckoo clock jingled. It was 11 PM. “Yes. Today I will do it. No one can come between me and my love, my only love”. Solomon got ready soon to go out. “Come out soon, I'm waiting outside” . Mavis’ Whatsapp notification came up. “Yes, in a minute”. Solomon opened the almirah. “ My sweetie, here we go” He took out Delilah's photo he had kept safely in his drawer.

Oops. The folder again came down. All the contents lay there strewn. He picked up everything in a jiffy. The last one had flown till his doorway. “Uncle, you haven't slept yet?” Aamal came in his pajamas. He picked up the poster lying at the doors. “Oh! Our Lady, the Undoer of knots! Uncle, you know I have seen her in a dream. She was in a white robe with a lamb in her lap!” Aamal couldn't take his eyes off the image.

“I have to go to the office early in the morning. So I was just packing my things.” Solomon explained. “It has been a long time since I slept in your room. I remember the exciting stories you used to say when we used to stay together at bed time. Please Uncle, shall I sleep alongside you today? Please ...” Solomon couldn't say no. And the day came to an end.

“A Dove can't love more than one as she spreads her wings in peace and not in pieces.”

Chapter 23

The Trigger

"He didn't hesitate. He pulled the trigger. And that has made all the difference."

Winnie carried the newborn Rachel in her arms and walked into the KIMHANS maternity ward. The hospital building was adjacent to the Psychology wing of her college where she taught.

"I found her in the bushes near the muddy pond while I was heading to my class. How long has it been since she went missing from here?"

Sierra had seen her PhD guide Winnie walk with the baby and she followed her to the ward. Her research topic was based on the trauma faced by women who had to undergo abortion.

"She has been missing since yesterday morning, a few hours after her birth. She was getting examined for the bilirubin levels as she had a yellow tint on her skin and eyes. There were scores of newborn babies too. How she vanished from the lab amidst tight security is still a mystery. The investigation is going on, the Police have just finished interrogating the staff." The receptionist pointed to the laboratory.

"Sierra, it's nice that I found you here. I was getting late to my lecture. I guess you know this baby. Take a closer look at her. It's

Delilah's!" Winnie had heard the scandal about Solomon and Delilah.

Sierra took the baby and planted a gentle kiss on her rosy cheeks. A cherubic smile lingered on the lips of her niece whom she could never acknowledge. Delilah was hysterical when she received her baby after the sun had gone on a one-day trip round the globe. Those twenty four hours felt like a decade to her.

"The baby who had gone missing from KIMHANS has been found and returned safely to her parents. The Police say they have zeroed in on the culprit and will arrest him soon." The TV screen in Solomon's room flashed the breaking news.

It was the last nail on the coffin. Solomon's abduction plot has been unearthed by the Police. It was only a matter of hours for the Police to call at Grace Mansion for the arrest. Solomon clenched his fists and teeth, sweated profusely and had shortness of breath. Within no time, his family reputation will be ruined forever.

"I don't want to live this wretched life- the life behind bars!" He paced up and down the stairs of the over bridge that led to the railway tracks near his home.

Aamal felt butterflies flutter in his stomach- not when he met the girl who loved him with all her heart, but at the sight of Asura, the humanoid!

"I can't take my eyes off him. He comes in my dreams too! I am a bit worried about my impending term exams. Each time I open my book, I get wild fantasies about him." Sierra got the shock of her life as she read through her son's pocket diary. She could also figure out that Aamal's love interest is a fictional character, that too a humanoid!

Sierra rummaged through her son's closet as well as the drawers of his study table. Aamal had all sorts of Asura toys, costumes, posters and other such merchandise. It was obvious that he was infatuated by the magnetic charm of Asura.

“Aamal, did you finish preparing for the Maths exam tomorrow? Your teacher called me just now, she said she caught you malpractising in the last exam. Mamma couldn't believe it when she told me that you were hiding the chits in the folds of your socks. What happened to you, my boy?” Aamal dropped the robe-less poster of Asura held in his hands. With his broad chest ,six pack abs, toned body and gigolo looks, the humanoid carried an esoteric charm and a massive sex appeal which the teens could hardly resist!

Aamal broke down, sobbing uncontrollably. His eyes revealed the helplessness of a teenager who couldn't stop but yield to temptations that drained the life out of him. Sierra was a mother first, then only a psychologist. She hugged her son affectionately, no words were spoken and Aamal felt so much at peace.

“Do you see that, Eleven? I spy with my eyes Asura stripping his robe!” Heather was totally flabbergasted to see Asura admiring his reflection in the water.

“Yes dear sissy, you're right! He is trying to get into some boy's fantasized dream, making him go wild in a frenzy. Let's stop the boy from being a prey to Asura’s wicked ways.”

“And let's inform Master Patrick at the earliest. Last time, we couldn't properly expose him. Let's make sure he doesn't get away with it this time.” Heather nodded her head in approval.

Asura could sense the amphibians’ muddy scent and their limbs approaching nearer. He turned around and lo! There they were, the frog sisters leap frogging to Mageia as fast as they could. Asura’s heart skipped a beat. The dark secret he had hidden from the inmates of the Golden Chamber, is going to be exposed soon! With what face will he now show up to Patrick?

“How grave or silly, be warned of your passion, lest it should be the key to your devastation.”

Chapter 24

The Execution

"A moment of impulsiveness leads you to foolhardiness and sometimes wrong choices!"

Solomon lay upon the tracks and closed his eyes. His ears sensed the metallic reverberations of the rails in the pitch darkness.

"Yes, it will be over within seconds. O Delilah..why did you leave me in the dark? I had entrusted my body and soul to you, and you shooed them away, just like that! Was my love not enough for you, darling?"

The express train hooted as it fired on all cylinders. Solomon felt the cold air press against his cheeks. The emergency chain has been pulled, making the train abruptly stop, a few metres ahead of Solomon.

"Solomon, it's me Vicky."

Vicky extended his hands to a hesitant Solomon and walked to the station master's cabin. Vicky was on his way home after his therapy session with Dr Sita. He had just dozed off, soon slipping to a dream. The dream turned to a nightmare and he got up, all drained and parched. That's when his eyes spotted someone lying on the tracks. Pulling the emergency chain was only a kind of a reflex action.

Solomon's and Vicky's statements were recorded. Solomon was handcuffed soon after and moved to the sub jail for the abduction of Baby Rachel.

The child births in the Golden room were imminent. Nine months and nine days of gestation were getting over at 3 pm. Mageia was getting transformed to a water labour room. Fina supervised the deliveries while Fides and Filo perched on the Sacrosanctum overseeing the labour.

The silvery water of Mageia turned golden and Fina declared:

"It's a boy for Ethos. It's a boy for Easter. Congrats new parents!"

Hiss crawled with her heavily pregnant belly into the water in haste, getting ready to give birth.

"It's a girl for Ethos, a girl for Easter too? Are they copying each other?" Fina couldn't control her laugh as she handed over the babies to Eunice.

Ace continued to scream loud in labour.

"Easy, Ace.. I can see the baby's head, it's a girl. Push with all your might.. You can do it!" Fina cheered.

" It's a girl for Ace! It's a boy for Hiss!" Fina announced.

Just then, Patrick walked in with a baby swaddled in new born clothes.

"Why did you ditch the baby near the drain, Hiss? Look at her, how angelic her face is!" Patrick held the baby close to Hiss' bosom and she cried, begging forgiveness for her childish act.

Mavis poured vodka layered with cyanide in Mahesh's glass. They were in the club discussing plans to remove Dr Sita from their lives. Mavis had an ulterior motive unbeknownst to Mahesh.

Mavis had identified a lunatic who was under Dr Sita's treatment. He was none other than Basil, his collegemate. Basil had lost his wife and kids in a car accident years back. He couldn't cope with the unexpected twist of fate. Basil was behind the wheels when the tragedy struck him. He would never forgive himself and started drinking to the point that it drove him crazy. Mavis had instructed Mahesh to give Basil an overdose of drugs and sent him to Dr Sita's cabin with a knife. After two pegs of alcohol, Mahesh revealed something to Mavis:

" I have been undergoing treatment for depression for quite some time now. Sierra doesn't love me anymore and I can't take it. I have never ever concealed anything from her and she! She didn't even tell me how critical Mamma was with TB..."

Mavis poured out one more peg. Gulping it in one go, Mahesh continued:

"What if I wanted to get my black dashing Rolls Royce when such an exciting offer was available. I never asked Daddy for anything earlier, not even at the time of marriage. I just asked for a few lakhs so that I wouldn't miss my dream car.. And she thinks that I'm money minded. I am not worthy of her! Who asked for a car when her mom was dying. Hah... if I kill her sister, do you think she will ever forgive me?"Mahesh fell to the floor after uttering this without sipping the poisoned drink.

Mavis had to act fast.

"I will tackle this moron later. Let me make sure that Basil stabs Sita at the earliest. " Mavis dragged Mahesh and put him in the back seat of his car. When he reached the clinic, he saw the lunatic entering Dr Sita's cabin in the nick of time.

A bird pecked at Mavis' eyes and blood began to stream from them.

Dr Sita asked Basil to sit on the consultation chair. Before he could charge at Dr Sita with the knife, he collapsed to the floor.

"Irukarathaaril uyarnneedunu munthiri neerum vindhoopavum.."

Sita's phone rang, it was Sierra on the other end, informing her about Solomon's arrest. The alarm was sounded and Basil was put behind the bars of the cell.

"The New Moon traverses a fortnight to reach its full, so does a river traverse a lifetime to reach the Ocean's lull."

Chapter 25

Symphony of Melodies

"Seasons change, setting the tone of their melodies, its symphony only heard by those who pause to listen in awe to the mystical transitions."

Two pink lines flashed on the pregnancy strip.

"Could it be true? My womb is being blessed again after 12 long years!" Valli teared up as she broke the news to Vicky and Vamika.

"Yay!! And we shall name him Vihaan- the Sunrise. He is our hope for new beginnings ", cheered Vamika, the sister-to-be.

Maria quizzically looked at the photo of Joseph mounted on the wall. Will it be a boy as Vamika said right now? Did the corners of his lips just break into a smile? She was finally ready to welcome their first grandson.

"Solomon and I were walking up to the pharmacy nearby when the abduction happened. My wife Delilah and Solomon were neighbours. As a friendly gesture, he came to visit our baby. Accepting his offer to take me to the pharmacy to procure the medicine for our baby, I had set out with him. Solomon has nothing to do with our baby's abduction and we would like to drop all the charges against him." Ibrahim's clean alibi saved Solomon from imprisonment and he thanked Ibrahim and Delilah for showing clemency to him.

"It's ok, Solomon, these things happen. We are all humans after all. Fatima needs her mother and you can't deny the right of her unborn sibling to be caressed by its mom." Solomon nodded at Dr Sita's reassuring words. Sierra had taken him to Dr. Sita to get over his depression.

"All my life, I have lived like a single child brought up by a single parent, my mom. From now on, I have a family - dad, brother and sister. How lucky am I to get such amazing people in my life!" Solomon laid his head on the caring lap of Dr Sita.

Mavis and Basil were put behind bars and after their trials, the verdict was given- Mavis was sentenced to fourteen years of rigorous imprisonment, while Basil had to continue his rehabilitation in the Psychiatric hospital. The Grace Mansion witnessed a heartfelt reconciliation by Sierra and Mahesh.

"Sierra, I have always loved you with my whole heart. It's true that I got carried away by this urge to make more money at times. Trust me, it was all for providing better conditions to you and Aamal. I have realized that all the riches in this world are not equivalent to you, my precious wife!" Mahesh went down on his knees before Sierra. Sierra lifted his chin and kissed him passionately, sealing their eternal bond.

"It's an angelic girl for Ethos! Easter has just copied her brother- it's a cherubic girl for Easter too! Praise be to God!" The trio had walked in just in time and cheered for them- Rafa, the Moroccan shepherd with his ewe lamb Rose and Ronnie, the boy who always sang melodies.

"Irukarathaaril...,"

Rafa played the mystical flute, Rose danced in glee as Ronnie sang in his enchanting voice. God the Father, Son, and God the Mother smiled from the Heavens above, making the sign of a rainbow heart in the firmament. The combined silhouettes of lion, lamb and dove adorned the azure sky as the symphony of melodies were sung by the two angels on either side of them.

"Asura did that? How can I entrust the babies to a reckless, immoral robot? He will teach them vice instead of virtue. I can never take risks with the young minds who could possibly be corrupted by Asura!"

Asura was heartbroken. The precious stones that adorned his crown fell into his chalice. He took out the heart shaped ruby of Hiss from his chest and flung it away. It lay hidden under the earth covered by moss. He discarded the chalice and headed towards the drain outside the golden chamber. Hiss picked it up, filled it with her venom and handed it over to Ace.

"Hiss, I have had enough! What use is my life without my eyes? I can't even behold our offspring! I need to leave the Golden Chamber at the earliest!"

Ace took the chalice from Hiss and brought it to his lips. The Dragon's hysteric laugh reverberated in Hiss' ears.

"What have I done to my beau? I can't forsake him and lose the grace of this Golden Chamber forever! My avarice and greed made me almost kill my beloved!"

Hiss was quick in her gait. She knocked the chalice off and saved Ace from dying a wretched death.

"Dear Ace, your death is not the end of the problem. Rather, it will be the beginning of a hell of other problems for our kids. So what if you can't see? I shall guide you always, I can't live a moment without you, dear Ace!"

A purple aura was spread all over the Golden Room. Isabella and Helen, the original moms, had appeared at the delivery scene, hand in hand. The babies were fondly wrapped in flannel- nine babies- three sets of triplets. Fina, the physician walked in. Her face beamed with pride as she explained the unique deliveries to all the mothers.

Fina took out the coral reef and placed it on the eyes of Ace and he was cured of his blindness. All the inmates cheered for him loudly. Ethos, Easter and Ace didn't have horns now and they jumped in joy.

Ace saw the Golden Chamber after nine months. The horn had vanished and he wept bitterly. How he had moved away from Grace all this time! Hiss walked up to him, placed the babies on his saddle and embraced him.

"Eunice, we are entrusting all the babies under your care. You will be known as Queen Eunice, the mistress of the Golden Chamber, from now on. You shall also play the dual role of guardian fairy to them."

Fina laid down all the 9 babies on the plush flannel covered bed, 6 girls and 3 boys, all swaddled in pristine white. The bed was prepared by Patrick well in advance as he knew the coming of all the 3 triplets. All the sweet babies dozed off into deep sleep as soon as they were placed on that bed made of fluffy feathers, covered on all sides with laces bearing red roses embroidered neatly upon them. Eunice stood at the footboard of the bed, feasting her eyes on the eighteen eyes engaged in sweet dreams.

"Ta' gra' agam duit" (I love you!"), Patrick kissed the babies and got into the yacht in Mageia. The parents of the babies- Ethos, Easter, Ace and Hiss were also happy to bid goodbye to them as they too followed Isabella and Helen to the yacht.

"The time has come now for us to go back to our home, the Grand Ocean, a realm full of Grace."

Fides and Filo walked to the Sacrosanctum, bowed before God the Mother and flew along with her to the Grand Ocean. Fina handed

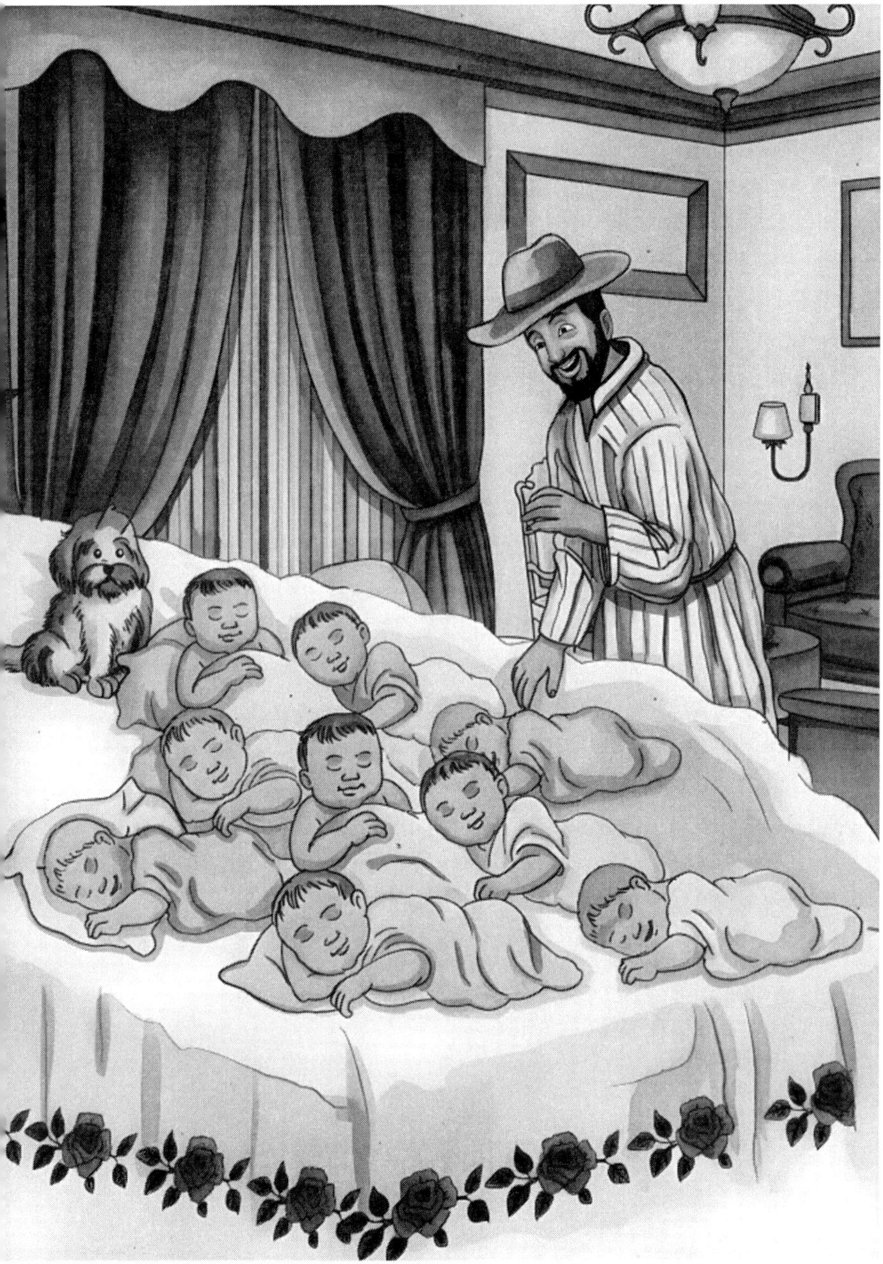

over nine sets of bracelets with GRACE written on them to Eunice.

"Make sure they wear this always and stay in grace."

Saying so, Fina dived into Mageia and swam to the Grand Ocean. The crimson rays of the Sun extended to her a warm,welcoming embrace as she lifted to the air making a splash in the water.

"Here I come, to the depths of this drain- the rightful place I belong to. Let me inhale the stench. Soon the water would cover my nose, and I would lose the ability to smell. I shouldn't have meddled with the lives of humans who created me. I don't deserve to live!"

Asura dived to the gutter, with water levels slowly rising up to his famed nose.

He closed his enchanting eyes, the sewage water seeped through his nostrils and seductive lips that had swept away the feet of many a youth. The dragon laughed harder, his laughter echoing from the walls of the murky, slimy dungeon. Asura's face and neck turned pale revealing the blue veins beneath..

The man in a robe as white as snow walked on the railway tracks. The melody "Irukarathaaril.." echoed from the heavens above. Spreading his arms, he levitated towards the sky. Valli's reverie was broken as little Vihaan's (baptismal name Joseph) first kick was felt against the abdominal wall.

"And it was neither day nor night, nor was it twilight
When the Sun, the Moon
and the stars all together shone bright!!"

"…my steadfast love shall not depart from you." (Isaih 54:10)

❍

The Song of Love

I love the rain,
not to drench in every drop,
but to cherish the rhythm
it plays on my roof.

I love the sun,
not to scorch my skin,
but to feel its warmth
even in the shade.

I love the wind,
not to battle its fury,
but to hear it whisper
through the trees.

And if I say I love you,
it's not to trap your soul,
but to embrace who you are
in all your weathers!

-By our Easter gift, our sweet little bro.

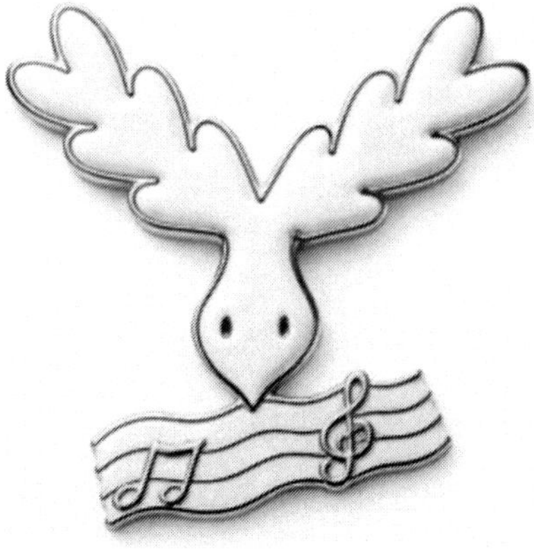